HOW TO
LIVE
THE
CHRISTIAN
LIFE

TERRY SIMPSON

ISBN 978-1-64670-909-0 (Paperback)
ISBN 978-1-64670-910-6 (Digital)

Covenant Books, Inc.
11661 Hwy 707
Murrells Inlet, SC 29576
www.covenantbooks.com

CONTENTS

INTRODUCTION

From beginning to end the Christian life is the best life that can be lived on this earth. I don't mean it is the most comfortable life that can be lived, or the easiest life or the most affluent or popular. But it is the best life and that is because it is Christ's life. The Christian life in lived in the power and purpose of the Lord Jesus Christ.

Paul was in chains before his earthly judge and his court and he said, "I wish that all of you here were as I am, except for these chains." But even in chains and in prison this man could write a book on joy and in it could say, "For me to live is Christ." Christ's life was one of fullness of the Spirit, even in the presence of His critics and crucifiers. God had set a table before Him in the presence of His enemies and for the joy set before Him He endured the cross.

Jesus calls on us to join Him in this best of all lives. He tells us how to live it and He shows us how. He said, "I have come that you might have life and have it more abundantly."

He offers that life, His life, as a gift to be received by anyone who will believe. He offers it to you. He said, "Come to Me all of you who labor and are heavy burdened and I will give you rest." Then He said, "Take My yoke upon you and learn of Me."

That is what we will be doing in this book,
learning from Jesus how to live the best life
possible, how to live the Christian life.

Welcome to life in all its fullness. Welcome to
abundant life. Welcome to Christ's life.

HOW TO LIVE THE CHRISTIAN LIFE

For me to live is Christ, and to die is gain.
—Philippians 1:21

This is the first installment in a series of lessons on how to live a godly life, which is the Christian life. The only godly life possible is the Christian life. Without Christ we don't know God, and we can't possibly live the Christian life (John 14:6). If you don't live the Christian life, then death will not be gain to you. In fact, it will be eternal loss. You will lose everything you have and spend eternity separated from Christ in the place Jesus called hell. *You must first become a Christian if you are to live the Christian life.* To do that you must give up your own life. Jesus said, "If anyone desires to come after me, let him deny himself and take up his cross and follow Me" (Luke 9:23).

You cannot live the Christian life if you don't first die to your self-life because the Christian life is a crucified and resurrected life. It is a miraculous life that gives you the ability to live for God with His resurrection power. You must die to your own life and be resurrected to Christ's life with Him as your Lord and Savior. This is a major problem for people today, because many have the wrong idea of the Christian life. They erroneously think that Christ comes into their lives to help them live their lives. You've got your own agenda, things you think are important, things you want to accomplish; and Christ can help you do all that. Wrong! That is a dangerous heresy, and those who believe that lie can never live the Christian life.

Christ comes into your life to help you live *His* life, with His agenda and purpose. He doesn't help you become a better person;

7

He enables you to become a different person. "If anyone is in Christ, he is a new creation; old things have passed away; behold, all things have become new" (2 Cor. 5:17). For years now I have asked people this simple question: Why did Jesus die and rise again? And I've never had even one person give me the scriptural answer I am going to show you right now. That's because they have swallowed the whole lie that Christ comes into our lives to help us live our lives with peace and joy. Here's the answer Paul gave to the question why Christ died: "He died for all, that those who live should live no longer for themselves, but for Him who died for them and rose again" (2 Cor. 5:15).

The Christian life is Christ's life. "For me to live is Christ (to live)," Paul wrote. The Christian life is not your life; it is His life, the Christ life. He lives His life through you. That's where the power over sin comes from and the power to do good. He is the reason we live and the motive behind everything the Christian does.

But *nobody lives this life perfectly.* That's because we are all still in our unredeemed bodies, called *the flesh,* which continually pulls us to live less than we ought, and because we are all ever growing, there are things we haven't learned yet. And make no mistake about it, you have to learn how to live the Christian life. None of this comes naturally to us. That is why we have a Bible, to teach us things we need to know.

Jesus said, "Take My yoke upon you and learn of Me" (Matt. 11:29). And He said in the Great Commission: "Go and make disciples, teaching them to observe all things I have commanded you" (Matt. 28:19–20). We have the greatest Teacher in the world (the Holy Spirit) and the greatest textbook in the world (the Holy Bible). With the help of these two necessary things, we can learn how to live the Christian life, which is the best life in or out of this world.

"For we all stumble in many things," James said in 3:2. When we were small, we stumbled and fell a lot. We were weak and unskilled. But as we grew older, we became stronger. We had to get back up and do it better until we stumbled less and less and could even go long periods of time without stumbling. What is true in the natural realm is true in the spiritual realm.

But this propensity to fail does not mean we can't have victory over the flesh. In fact, that's precisely what the gospel (which produces the Christian life) is all about. The normal Christian life is a life of power, victory, blessing, wisdom, holiness, truth, humility, and glory.

That is what we are going to be studying about: how to live the kind of life that brings the greatest blessings to us and to others. That's exactly how Jesus lived: He was the greatest blessing to others and consequently He was blessed beyond measure (Phil. 2:9–10). We want to be a blessing to God and bless others. We want to please God and be helpful to others. Who doesn't want that? A Christian certainly wants that. But we must set our minds and hearts and bodies to live it. "We make it our aim to be well pleasing to Him" (2 Cor. 5:9). Do you want to live a life fully pleasing to the Lord? Of course, you do. That's what these lessons are all about. The word for *aim* in that verse is very instructive. The old cowboy Westerns have people pulling their pistols and firing willy-nilly and hitting their targets almost without fail. That's why they called them gunslingers. But that's only in the movies. In truth, you only hit what you aim at. My dad took me hunting everything. I never knew how to shoot a gun until I went into the military, and that was mainly because my dad would shoot first, and when he was aiming at a duck or squirrel or whatever, he demanded no distractions—from me! I had to sit perfectly still as he took careful aim to hit whatever he was shooting at. No distractions. You pay no attention to anything else, or you miss your target. Paul said, "We make it our aim to be well pleasing to God."

We too must make it our aim. If we don't aim to please God, we won't please God. No distractions. That's why the Bible says, "Do not love the world, neither the things in the world…" (1 John 2:15). The world is a major distraction to keep us from aiming to please God. Aim, or you won't live the Christian life.

What we will be covering in this series of studies is how to live the life that is fully in the will of God. How to be a godly man. How to be a godly woman. How to be a godly child. How to live the life of a godly husband, a godly wife, a godly mom or dad, a godly young person, a godly church member, a godly neighbor. We will be exploring how to honor God with our lives and thus live the best life possible. But you have to want it. I mean, want it more than anything else. More than treasure or personal pleasure. You must want it as a deer pants for water. What we will learn is a panacea for everybody in all situations: heart, home, church, and work.

You can live a godly life if you are *poor*, but you can live a better godly life if you have all you need and enough to help others. You can live a godly life if you are *sick*, but you will live a better Christian life if you are well. This is the will of God: "That you may prosper in all things and be in health" (3 John 2). You can live a godly life without being perfect, but you can live a better life by having victory over your addictions and sins. It is God's will for you to live a powerful holy life, for you to live *the normal Christian life.*

Learning how to live the Christian life is a *panacea* for all of life. A panacea is "an answer or solution for all problems or difficulties." In the coming lessons we will learn many things, like how to live without worry. No Christian should ever worry about anything, because every Christian has a compassionate, almighty, sovereign Heavenly Father and thus has no reason to worry. We will learn how to be happy all the time (taken from this very first chapter in Philippians); how to get along with everybody all the time; how to have everything you need, how to prosper and be in health; how to get your prayers answered; how to have faith; how to live with peace of mind even when you're in the greatest storm of your life; how to handle temptation; how to deal with depression; deal with doubts, rejoice always, and much, much more.

This could be the greatest series of lessons you have ever learned, so don't miss one. First things first, the Christian life begins by becoming a Christian. That's a simple thing to take care of, and it's wrapped up in one word—commitment. You must by faith commit yourself to Christ as your Lord and Savior. Do that now! Commit your life and decide to live for the One who died that we should no longer live for ourselves but for Him who died and rose again. Commit. You can't live the Christian life if you don't commit your life to Christ.

HOW TO LIVE THE CHRISTIAN LIFE

Live by Faith

*Without faith it is impossible to please Him, for he
who comes to God must believe that He is,
and that He is a rewarder of those who diligently seek Him.*
—Hebrews 11:1–6

We can only live the Christian life as we live by faith in the word of God. The just are not to live by faith in their feelings, which can be soulish and undependable when it comes to matters of faith. Feelings are emotions, and they tend to be very fickle and unreliable. A lady once told me that another lady shared an interpretation of a dream and it devastated the one talking to me. I asked her why she had taken it so seriously, and she told me she had always considered the other lady a spiritual person. I told her that I had known that other lady for years and I had never considered her to be a spiritual person but that I considered her an emotional person. Spiritual and emotional are not the same. And we are not to live by faith in faith. That's ridiculous! We don't walk by sight, for there is truth that is beyond what we can see. Faith operates in the realm of the unseen. We can't live by faith in ourselves.

Our new school secretary where all the kids came all the time put a sign prominently on the top front of her desk that said, "Believe in Yourself." I told her to remove that from her office, and she was rather astounded that I didn't agree with that sentiment. I told her I would agree with it if I could find it in the Bible, which I could not, but I could find "Believe in Jesus" hundreds of times in the Bible, and that she should put that on her desk, which she did.

What we are to believe is the object of our faith, and that is God. I know it is extremely popular in sports to tell people they have to believe in themselves, but that's still not in the Bible. The Bible doesn't say, "I can do all things." It says, "I can do all things through Christ" (Phil. 4:13). The declaration of Scripture is, "The just shall live by faith" (Heb. 10:38), and that faith is in God and Jesus (John 14:1). It is not easy in this physical world to live by faith. That's why we need to be born again and need to learn how to operate by the spirit in faith.

A history lesson can show how important faith is. Out of the Dark Ages when the Catholic Church held the church in the darkness of ignorance and superstition, the Reformation emerged with the three revolutionary truths. Luther, Calvin, and other heralded these doctrines:

1. Only Christ. The Catholic Church taught that there were many mediators between us and God: Mary and a host of other saints they could pray to and get their requests to God. But the Reformers said, "For there is one Mediator between God and men, the Man Jesus Christ, who gave Himself a ransom for all" (1 Tim. 2:5). All believers need to get to God is Christ.

2. Only the Scriptures. The Catholics added their own writings to the canon of Scripture: decrees of the popes and writings of the church fathers that to them were just as binding and infallible as the Bible. Martin Luther said at his trial, "My mind is held captive to the word of God. So, help me God I can do none other." He had to escape from them for his life.

3. Only faith. The Catholics preached salvation by works: faith plus works, and that included even giving money to the church to pay for your sins (indulgences, they were

called) and help them build their expensive buildings in Rome. The Reformers said, "By grace we have been saved through faith, not of works lest any man should boast" (Eph. 2:8–9). They were right. It is by faith alone that we are saved and live. This is a cardinal doctrine of the church and the Holy Bible.

Since faith is so important to God and to our salvation from beginning to end, we should have a clear definition of it. *What is faith?* We are justified by faith, and we live by faith. So what is faith? First, faith is a noun. It is something, something tangible. The Bible definition is "Faith is the substance of things hoped for." But don't think of it as physical substance like the seat you sit in or the floor you stand on. Faith is substance in the spirit world. *It is a revelation made known to us by the Spirit of God through the Word or visions or dreams, and it comes with a divinely ordained response.* Faith cannot be separated from works. That's why the next statement in Hebrews 11:1 says, "Faith is the evidence of things not seen." The evidence is the action by those who have faith and live by faith. Believe is the verb that is the counterpart of faith, the opposite side of the coin; therefore, one doesn't come without the other. Faith believes, with action following.

Faith and obedience to that revelation are inseparable. You cannot say you have faith and not act on that faith. You can have faith but not the faith Christ authors. You cannot have faith without obedience. You can obey without having faith because you can mechanically do something without having faith. You can repeat a prayer without having faith in God. You can go through the motions without trusting God to fulfill His promises. For example, you can tithe without doing it in faith. That money may bless others, but it will not bring a blessing to you from God, for *without faith it is impossible to please God.*

Praying does no good unless we pray in faith. "If any of you lacks wisdom, let him ask of God, who gives to all liberally, and it will be given to him. But let him ask in faith, with no doubting...For let not that man suppose that he will receive anything form the Lord"

(James 1:5–7). And *"The prayer of faith shall save the sick"* (James 5:15). After the apostles saw the fig tree withered from the root up in just one day after Jesus cursed it, Jesus said, "Have faith in God." He explained to them that they could do the works of God if they would simply have faith in God and believe what He told them to say and that He would answer their prayers (Mark 11:20–24).

And *hearing* the word of God does not benefit us unless we hear with faith. Referring to the wilderness wanderers, Hebrews 4:2 says, "The word which they heard did not profit them, not being mixed with faith in those who heard it." James says, "Faith without works is dead. Was not Abraham our father justified by works when he offered Isaac on the altar? Likewise, was not Rahab the harlot also justified by works when she received the messengers and sent them out another way?" (2:20–21, 25). These acts of obedience were the evidence of things not seen. Abraham acted on the word he got from God. Rahab acted on the word she heard about what God had done for the Israelites. The results justified their confidence in the word of God.

James wrote that "Faith without works is dead." When James talked about works, he was not talking about the works of the law. How do I know that? Because the two examples he gave of faith were in violation of the law: God told Abraham to sacrifice his son and Rahab lied to the sheriff (2:21, 25). The work is the very thing God revealed for you to do or the action that shows you believe what God said.

Every character in Hebrews 11 who had faith and did something:

> *By faith Abel offered to God a more accept-*
> *able sacrifice, by faith Noah prepared an ark, by*
> *faith Abraham obeyed, by faith Isaac blessed Jacob,*
> *by faith Joseph made mention of the departure of*
> *the children of Israel and gave instructions concern-*
> *ing his bones, by faith Moses refused to be called*
> *the son of Pharaoh's daughter, choosing rather to*
> *suffer affliction, by faith he forsook Egypt, by faith*
> *they passed through the Red Sea, through faith they*

subdued kingdoms, worked righteousness, obtained promises, stopped the mouths of lions, wandered about in sheep skins, being destitute, afflicted and tormented.

And that is only to mention a few of them. Faith works.

Secondly, *the faith that Jesus authors never ends.* Faith always obtains the promise. Jesus is the author and finisher of our faith (Heb. 12:2). "*These all died in faith*" is the point of Hebrews 11, coming out of the last verses of chapter 10, "The just shall live by faith; but if anyone draws back, My soul has no pleasure in him." Faith finishes. All true believers endure to the end. These OT characters did. Every one of them did. Even though they had lapses of faith, their faith endured to the end. David messed up and so did Samson and the others, but they died in faith. The funny thing about this is, not all these believers died and yet it says they all died in faith. The point is, every one of these who had faith lived by it till they were seen no more. Enoch didn't die, but he was last seen walking by faith.

The rubber meets the road when you think of those you know who do not live by faith but yet claim to have faith. They appear to have formerly lived by faith, but no more. They no longer read the Bible, have no prayer life to speak of, have forsaken the assembly of believers, do not make disciples, and the list goes on. They are not living by faith. These people "have need of endurance," but they appear to have none. They have "drawn back to perdition, and God finds no pleasure in them." How diligent should we be to have compassion on them and encourage them to repent and make their calling and election sure? We must love them enough to tell them to "lay aside every weight and the sin which so easily ensnares us," and look unto Jesus.

A good scriptural example goes a long way to show something because the things that happened to those in the Old Testament happened for our admonition and learning. In 2 Chronicles 20:1–30, we have the story of King Jehoshaphat and Jerusalem and Judah being attacked by three huge armies. This good king shows us that people who walk by faith are not immune to attacks. If you are never assaulted by the devil, you are not walking by faith. If you never meet the enemy coming toward and against you, maybe it's because you are going in the same direction. The king made the appropriate spiritual response: he called for an assembly at the house of God, fasted, and prayed. When you are under attack, call the brethren together to pray with you. Go to the house of God and seek the Lord together. The king's prayer is an incredible prayer of faith (v. 6–12) where he appeals to the promises of God, the glory and reputation of God because He had identified Himself with them. He acknowledged God's sovereignty (v. 6), covenant (v. 7), presence (v. 8–9), goodness (v. 10), and possession (v. 11), and their utter dependence on Him (v. 12). Faithful people must pray the prayer of faith. Judah did and look what God did. Faith is the victory that overcomes the world. Faith always wins in the end.

"Then the Spirit of the Lord came upon Jahaziel and the Lord said, 'Do not be afraid nor dismayed because of this great multitude, for the battle is not yours, but God's'" (v. 15). Somebody needs to hear from God and speak for God. We will remain in fear until the word of God comes to us. Faith is the opposite of fear. Fear is actually faith in the enemy, but faith looks to God. Ten spies looked at the giants and were afraid to enter the land, but two looked at God and voted to go in. Fear will keep you from faith, so God tells them to let fear go. Then He instructs them to go out against them and He would be with them and fight for them (v. 16–17).

Faith lives by prayer, by the word, by worship (v. 18–19). That is the life of faith. That is how we live by faith. They did what God had said. Check this out: "So they rose early in the morning and went out…Jehoshaphat stood and said, 'Believe in the Lord and you shall be established; believe in His prophets and you shall prosper.'" So they went out with the choir leading them! Much like He did with Gideon's enemies (Judg. 17:15–23), God confounded the enemy armies and they all killed each other. Israel took a great spoil, and they came back the same way they went out—singing praises to God. Faith sings. Paul and Silas sang praises to God in prison. That was the faith they lived by, and God fought for them too. He will fight for all those who live by faith. The battle belongs to those who have faith in God. So live by faith and live in victory and joy!

We sing praise songs in every worship service. Why do you think we do that? Just tradition? No! We do that because great victories are won while we are singing praises to God. When God is being praised, demons flee, if we are singing in faith! If you just stand there mouthing words and not believing what you are singing, the music and singing might sound good, but it profits you nothing. Those praises sung to God must be mixed with faith, and when they are, your enemies flee and God gives you the victory. *Faith is the victory that overcomes the world* (1 John 5:4).

HOW TO LIVE THE
CHRISTIAN LIFE

Hearing the Word of God

Faith comes by hearing and hearing by the word of God.
—Romans 10:17

Recently, I gave three lessons on speaking the word of God. All God's works are voice activated, and God uses our voice to activate them. In this study I want to emphasize the other side of speaking the word—hearing the word. We don't need to speak the word until after we have heard the word. Don't be saying things for God that you haven't heard from God.

We cannot be saved without hearing the word of God. We are saved by faith, and faith comes by hearing the word. It is the word of God that brings first the hearing ear and then the word that is to be heard in order to be saved. *We begin the Christian life by hearing the word of God and we continue in it the same way.* Jesus said, "My sheep hear My voice and I know them, and they follow Me, and I give to them eternal life" (John 10:27–28). Those who belong to Christ are the ones who hear His voice.

Jesus said, "If anyone has ears to hear, let him hear" (Mark 4:23). I assume all the people He was talking to had physical appendages attached to the sides of their heads. His sheep hear His voice with their inner ears, their spirit ears, their hearts. Jesus said, "He who is of God hears God's words; therefore, you do not hear, because you are not of God" (John 8:47). The *hears* here is present tense, meaning he who is of God is hearing (continues to hear) God's words. This is how you know you belong to God—you are hearing God's words.

"If you continue in My word then are you truly My disciples" (John 8:31). Jesus emphasizes the need to continue in His word, not just to receive it once. He also said, "We live by every word that proceeds from the mouth of God" (Matt. 4:4). How many words? Every word. We must never stop hearing and doing the word of God if we hope to be His true disciples.

The importance of hearing and continuing to hear the word of God cannot be overstated. Once Jesus was teaching some hard things with His words and "from that time many of His disciples went back and walked with Him no more. Then Jesus said to the twelve, 'Do you also want to go away?' Then Simon Peter answered Him, 'Lord, to whom shall we go? You have the words of eternal life" (John 6:66–68). Make sure you never go back. Stop listening to His words, and you won't be hearing the words of eternal life.

You are going to live by somebody's words; either the devil (drugs, astrology, etc.), the world (music, entertainers, philosophies, etc.), or your own (thoughts, reasonings, etc); but you will live according to somebody's words. Why not live by Jesus's words? He alone has the words of eternal life. If you're going to be saved, if you're going to reach heaven, you'd better listen to God and keep listening to God. Tragically, many people will listen to the word of their friends and family rather than God's.

Carnal people will always listen to people rather than God. They live their lives by what others say instead of what God says. The words of friends and family carry more weight than the very words of God. If you're going to listen to someone, listen to someone who is on fire for God and will speak the words of God to you and not the words of unbelief. "You don't have to go to church to be a good Christian." That is not the word of God. That's a lie. The word of God says, "*The Lord added to the church those who were being saved; and they continued steadfast in the apostle's doctrine and in fellowship. So continuing daily with one accord...*" (Acts 2:42–47). The word of

19

God tells us, "Not forsaking the assembling of ourselves together, as the manner of some is" (Heb.10:25).

If you are going to be saved by faith, then know this: "Faith comes by hearing and hearing by the word of God" (Rom. 10:17). Faith does not come by having heard the word; it comes by hearing. That's present tense. "Today if you will hear His voice, harden not your heart" (Heb. 3:15). We must keep on hearing, believing, and obeying. We are born again by the word of God (1 Pet. 1:23) and by it we grow to maturity: "As newborn babes, desire the pure milk of the word, that you may grow thereby" (1 Pet. 2:2).

The word of God is divided into two kinds: there is the word that is *spoken and heard*, and there is the word that is *written* in the Bible. Both are the word of God, and both are essential to live the Christian life. The spoken and heard word is from two Greek words: *logos* and *rhema*. Both mean the same thing: the spoken and heard word of God. Jesus is called the logos, which means He is the personification and manifestation of the spoken word of God: "And the Word was made flesh" (Gen. 1:3–26; John 1:1–3, 14).

The other word is *graphe*, meaning the Scriptures: "All Scripture is given by inspiration of God…" (2 Tim. 3:16). This is *the prophetic word that came by holy men of God who spoke as they were moved by the Holy Spirit* (2 Pet. 1:19–21). Both of these are seen in John 2:22: "And the disciples believed the Scripture and the word which Jesus had said." They believed both the graphe (the word written of Him) and the logos (the word spoken by Him).

By about five to one the Bible emphasizes the word of God spoken and heard over the word written: 236 times to 51 times. The preponderance of Scriptures is overwhelming in emphasizing the importance of hearing.

When Moses, the original prophet, spoke the word to the ancient Hebrews in Deuteronomy 28, he said something very important. He identified the two types of the word of God and told them they would be blessed or cursed according to their relationship with the word. "If you will diligently obey the voice of the Lord your God, to observe carefully all His commandments, which I command you today, that the Lord will set you high above all nations of the earth. And all these blessings shall come upon you and overtake you, because you obey the voice of the Lord your God" (v. 1–2). Note carefully the two kinds of words here: the voice of God and the commandments of Moses that were written by God. Until Moses there was no written word of God, only the spoken word. Abraham had no Bible, but he walked with God.

The written word is given to ensure that what we hear from the spirit world is actually the voice of God. In Acts 17:10–12 the Bereans were more *fair-minded* than the Thessalonians, who had previously persecuted the missionary team, because when they heard Paul preach, "they received the word (logos) with all readiness and searched the Scriptures (graphe) daily to find out whether these things were so." They heard the word and then searched the Bible to see if what Paul was preaching and what they were hearing was indeed the word of God.

We hear a word and receive it in our spirits, then we either recall the word of God stored in our minds through previous study of the Bible or we get our Bibles out and see if what we heard is consistent with the Scriptures. We know by our spirits, but we understand with our minds that have been renewed by the word of God. The spirit is for hearing, knowing, and believing; the mind is for understanding and recalling. Both are helpful, even necessary to live the Christian life. Jesus said, "It is the Spirit who gives life; the flesh profits nothing. The words that I speak to you are spirit and they are life. But there are some of you who do not believe" (John 6:63–64).

Some believe with the flesh—that is, with their brains, and it does not benefit them. They are soulish believers and have no life in their spirits because they have not heard the word with their hearts. Christians believe because they have heard the word in their spirits from the voice of the Holy Spirit through the preached word. The distance between heaven and hell is the distance between your head and your heart. Are you hearing the word with your heart?

Like I said, by far the Bible gives the overwhelming emphasis to the spoken and heard word of God. Examples of the spoken word abound. "Speak the word only and my servant will be healed. When evening had come, they brought to Him many who were demon-possessed. And He cast out the spirits with a word and healed all who were sick" (Matt. 8:8, 16). When Jesus explained the parable of the seed and the soils (Mark 4:9, 14–20), He used a certain phrase four times. He had said, "He who has ears to hear let him hear." Then came this phrase: "When they hear…" All the soils (soils representing their hearts) heard the word. That's the point: the word comes by hearing. Profit from the word comes when the word heard is mixed with faith (Heb. 4:2).

Do you want to have faith? Then hear the word of the Lord. Do you want to have the Holy Spirit come to you? Then hear the word of God. "While Peter was still speaking these words, the Holy Spirit fell upon all those who heard the word" (Acts10:44). To be filled with the Spirit is to "let the word of Christ live in you" (Col. 3:16). The word there is logos, the spoken and heard word of God, not the Scripture. The Bible will tell you if what you're hearing in your spirit is the word of God or not, but we all need to be hearing the word because *it is the heard word that brings the faith and life.*

This is why we have the preaching of the word in all our worship services, virtually every time we get together. "God manifested His word through preaching," Paul wrote (Tit.1:3). Check this out: "For since, in the wisdom of God, the world through wisdom did not know God, it pleased God through the foolishness of the message preached to save those who believe" (1 Cor. 1:21). As foolish as it may seem, God saves people through the preaching of His word, if "we preach Christ crucified, the power of God and the wisdom of God" (1 Cor. 1:23–24).

The word (rhema) is near you, even in your mouth and in your heart (that is, the word of faith which we preach)" (Rom. 10:8). We are saved by the word of faith that is preached to us. *The just shall live by faith in the word of God that is being heard.* Isaiah spoke for God and said, "Incline your ear and come to Me. Hear and our souls shall live" (55:3). Hear the word and your soul shall live. Let's be hearing. Hear the word of God.

HOW TO LIVE THE CHRISTIAN LIFE

Hearing the Word of God
(Part 2)

Every Christian wants to know above everything else how to live the life he or she has been given by Christ. How to live the Christian life is the most important thing you will ever learn. We are in the beginning stages of learning what the Bible says about how to live the Christian life.

To live the life, we must be led by the Holy Spirit, who gave us the life and is the power and wisdom behind it. If you are not being led by the Spirit, you are not a child of God. It's that simple. I'm not making that up; the Bible says so: "For as many as are led by the Spirit, these are the sons of God" (Rom. 8:14). Jesus said, "My sheep hear My voice, I know them and they follow Me; and I give to them eternal life" (John 10:27–28). You can't follow Jesus without hearing His voice and if you don't follow Jesus, you are not one of His sheep and you don't have eternal life. Being led by the Spirit and hearing the word of God are not optional in the Christian life. They are the two tracks laid down by Jesus that lead to heaven. We must hear the word of God.

There are two heresies (false teachings) about in our day that are destroying many souls. One is that Jesus comes into your life to help you live your life, to help you live a better life with peace and joy. Nothing could be further from the truth. He doesn't come to give you a better life; He comes to give you a different life—His life with His agenda and purpose. He lifts us up to Him. This heresy denies the very purpose of the gospel and the meaning of salvation. "He died for all, that those who live should live no longer for themselves, but for Him who died for them and rose again" (2 Cor. 5:15). And "If anyone is in Christ, he is a new creation; old things pass away and all things become new" (2 Cor. 5:17). This destructive heresy destroys the necessity of repentance and conversion.

The second lie is that all you must do to follow Jesus and end up in heaven is to begin to follow Him. You don't have to continue following Him; all you need to do to win the race is begin the race. This is utter nonsense, and it denies the biblical doctrines of sanctification and the perseverance of the saints. Jesus said, "He who endures to the end shall be saved" (Matt. 24:13). And Hebrews 11:13 says, "These all died in faith." People think that starting the race is all that is necessary. This is so wrong. Don't believe it.

Don't believe either of these destructive heresies. "For you have need of endurance, so that after you have done the will of God, you may receive the promise" (Heb. 10:36). So continue to be led by the Spirit and continue to hear the word of God.

We begin the Christian life by hearing the word of God, and we continue in it the same way. It is by the word of God that the Christian life *commences*, and it is by listening to the word of God that the Christian life *continues*. Jesus said, "If you continue in My word then are you truly My disciples" (John 8:31). Jesus emphasizes the need to continue in His word, not just to receive it once. He also said, "*We live by every word that proceeds from the mouth of God*" (Matt. 4:4). How many words? Every word. We must never stop hearing and doing the word of God if we hope to be His true disciples.

The importance of hearing and continuing to hear the word of God cannot be overstated. Once Jesus was teaching some hard things with His words and "from that time many of His disciples went back and walked with Him no more. Then Jesus said to the twelve, 'Do you also want to go away?' Then Simon Peter answered Him, 'Lord, to whom shall we go? You have the words of eternal life" (John 6:66–

68). Make sure you never go back. Stop listening to His words, and you won't be hearing the words of eternal life. Carnal people always listen to people rather than God. Make sure you are not one of them.

"Faith comes by hearing and hearing by the word of God" (Rom. 10:17). Faith does not come by having heard the word; it comes by hearing. That's present tense. "Today if you will hear His voice, harden not your heart" (Heb. 3:15). We must keep on hearing, believing, and obeying. We are born again by the word of God: "Having been born again, not of corruptible seed but incorruptible, through the word of God" (1 Pet. 1:23). The corruptible seed is the word of men whose words will pass away with them. And it is by the word of God that we grow to maturity: "As newborn babes, desire the pure milk of the word, that you may grow thereby" (1 Pet. 2:2).

I'm talking about the spoken and heard word of God here. We need the spoken and the written word. The Bible is the word of God. But you can read the Bible all day long and get zero out of it if God doesn't speak to your heart, if you don't hear His voice inside of you. We must be led by the Spirit, and we must hear His voice.

Here's how this works and why it is so important. We hear a word and receive it in our spirits, then we either *recall* the word of God stored in our minds through previous study of the Bible or we get our Bibles out and *research* if what we heard is consistent with the Scriptures. We know by our spirits, but we understand with our minds that have been renewed by the word of God. The spirit is for hearing, knowing, and believing; the mind is for understanding and recalling. Both are helpful, even necessary to live the Christian life. Jesus said, "It is the Spirit who gives life; the flesh profits nothing. The words that I speak to you are spirit and they are life. But there are some of you who do not believe" (John 6:63–64). Some believe with the flesh—that is, with their minds only, and it does not benefit them. They are soulish believers and have no life in their spirits because they have not heard the word with their hearts. Christians believe because they have heard the word in their spirits from the voice of the Holy Spirit through the preached word. The distance between heaven and hell is the distance between your head and your heart. Are you hearing the word with your heart?

The importance of the spoken and heard word is found throughout the Bible. The prophet Ezekiel was told, "Prophesy to these bones and say to them, 'O dry bones hear the word of the Lord!'" (37:1–10). "He sent His word and healed them and delivered them from their destructions" (Ps. 107:20).

And we have this incident in the NT: a centurion said to Jesus, "Speak the word only and my servant will be healed. When evening had come, they brought to Him many who were demon-possessed. And He cast out the spirits with a word and healed all who were sick" (Matt. 8:8, 16). When Jesus explained the parable of the seed and the soils (Mark 4:9, 14–20), He used a certain phrase four times. He had said, "He who has ears to hear let him hear." Then came this phrase: "When they hear…" All the soils (soils representing people's hearts) heard the word. That's the point: the word comes by hearing. Profit from the word comes when the word heard is mixed with faith (Heb. 4:2).

Isaiah spoke for God and said, "Incline your ear and come to Me. Hear and our souls shall live" (55:3). Hear the word and your soul shall live. Let's be hearing. Hear the word of the Lord.

Now for the conclusion. Two things we all need to ask ourselves after we have heard the preaching:

1. *What is God saying to me through this word?* (I am listening. What is He saying?)
2. *What does God want me to do with what I have heard?* (How can I best obey this word?)

What I have tried to say to you in this word is, nothing is more important than hearing the word.

So don't miss an opportunity to hear. Do whatever you have to do to get under the sound of Bible preaching. It will feed your soul and cause you to grow. Get those you love under the preaching and teaching of the word. Do them a huge favor: invite them to listen, to come, and partake.

HOW TO LIVE THE
CHRISTIAN LIFE

Obey the Word of God

Be doers of the word and not hearers only, deceiving yourselves.
—James 1:22

W e see some vitally important things about the word of God in the first chapter of James, the most practical book of the New Testament. "Of His own will He brought us forth (birthed us) by the word of truth. Therefore, lay aside all filthiness and overflow of wickedness, and receive with meekness the implanted word, which is able to save your souls" (James 1:18, 21). It was God's sovereign will that caused us to be born again, and He used His word of truth (the gospel) to get the job done. We were dead in sin, God spoke to our hearts, and we became alive. He looked at us in our grave and said, "Live!" and our spirit came alive. Nobody ever conceived or birthed himself: "Who were born, not of blood, nor of the will of the flesh, nor of the will of man, but of God" (John1:13). Next, having laid aside the "earwax" (*filthiness*) of our moral wickedness, we are to receive with humility the word of God that is able to save our souls. Verse 18 speaks of regeneration and verses 21 to 22 speak of sanctification.

Our spirits being saved (birthed) is solely the act of the sovereign Spirit of God using the word of God, but our souls being saved is a matter of us cooperating with the word we hear. We can't receive the implanted word if we do not hear it. This is what is able to save our *souls*.

First, we must get rid of all impediments to hearing and then receive the word. *Meekness* means we receive the word with the attitude that we know nothing except what God tells us and we only hear what He says to us. If we listen to others who contradict God's word, our souls will not be saved. Then we must obey the word we have heard. If we don't obey the word, it will have no effect in our lives. We will not be blessed (v. 25). The deception is thinking we are living the Christian life when we are not obeying God's implanted word.

This simple fact is missed by so many. After over forty-nine years of pastoring, it is my firm conviction that many people come to church and it never enters their minds to actually do what the preacher preaches. They have no intention of obeying the word they hear. This is what the prophet was told by God in Ezekiel 33:30–33:

> Your people are talking about you to one another saying, "Please come and hear what the word is that comes from the Lord." So they come to you as people do, they sit before you as My people, and they hear your words, but they do not do them; for with their mouth they show much love, but their hearts pursue their own gain. Indeed, you are to them as a very lovely song of one who has a pleasant voice and can play well on an instrument, for they hear your words but they do not do them.

They were hearers of the word but not doers, and God said that His judgment would fall upon those who hear but don't do.

And it is what Paul talked to Timothy about when he wrote, "Take heed to yourself and to the doctrine. Continue in them, for in doing this you will save both yourself and those who hear you" (1 Tim. 4:16). Doctrine is what the word says on any given subject such as prayer, God, sin, Satan, faith, etc. The pastor preaches the word, and that word he preaches is the word that will save you. But it will only save you if you *do* it!

One more passage to underscore the importance of doing the word. Jesus preaches His famous Sermon on the Mount in Matthew 5–7, and He ends it in a very profound and practical way (7:21–27): "Not everyone who says to Me, 'Lord, Lord,' shall enter the kingdom of heaven, but he who *does* the will of My Father in heaven." Jesus proceeds to tell the stories about the two houses. The house represents a religious life; the rain represents divine judgment. We must do what the word of God says or divine judgment will fall on us.

Things that will keep you from obeying after you have heard are given to us by Jesus in His parable of the soils (Mark 4:13–20). Jesus had a huge following, but He knew the fallacy of large crowds: not everyone who hears the word will obey the word and bear the fruit of it. Some are so busy, the devil snatches the word immediately from their hearts. Gone before they can apply it. Then there are those with a shallow commitment, those who let the cares of this life, the deceitfulness of riches and desire for other things kill the word. As powerful as the heard word is, without bearing the fruit of it, we are not benefited by it. We heard and didn't do.

Hear the word of the Lord, believe the word, and obey the word. That is the Christian life. That is how we live the Christian life. Hear with faith and do what He says. When you come to church, have you set your mind to hear everything God has to say to you? Are you hanging on every word? And are you believing it with all your heart as though it is the word of God? And are you leaving this place and doing what you have heard?

It would be extremely helpful if at the close of every word you hear you ask God two questions:

1. *What are You saying to me in this message?* (What is the word You have for me here?)
2. *What do want me to do as a result of what I have heard from the word?* (What response should I make to what I have heard? How can I obey what God is saying to me?)

HOW TO LIVE THE CHRISTIAN LIFE

Avoid Legalism

*Judge not, that you be not judged. For with what
judgment you judge, you will be judged; and with the
measure you use, it will be measured back to you.*
—Matthew 7:1–3

*Who are you to judge another's servant? Or why do you show
contempt for your brother? For we shall all stand before the judgment
seat of Christ. Therefore, let us not judge one another anymore.*
—Romans 14:3–13

*Do not speak evil of one another, brethren. Whoever
speaks evil of his brother, judges his brother.*
—James 4:11

*For judgment is without mercy to the one who has
shown no mercy. Mercy triumphs over judgement.*
—James 2:13

*Whatever we ask we receive from Him, because we keep His
commandments and do those things that are pleasing in His
sight. This is His commandment: that we should believe on
the name of His Son Jesus Christ and love one another.*
—1 John 3:2–23

Avoid legalism. Avoid it like the plague. Run from it like Joseph did from Potiphar's wife. Legalism is the scourge of the earth and the curse of the church and of every Christian life. Legalism killed Jesus and persecuted Paul his whole life. You cannot live the Christian life and live by the law, for the same way we began the life (by grace) is the same way we must live it. Not only is the *commencement* of the Christian life obtained by grace, the *continuance* of it is no less by grace alone.

Nothing will keep you from living the Christian life like placing yourself and others under the law. You cannot live the Christian life and live under the law. It's either lived by grace and faith or the law, and it's not law. Any law, Old or New Testament. Law is law. We either will live by the law of God or the grace of God. The Christian life is living in the grace of God. What's to keep someone from living in sin? Not the law! Only grace saves from sin and puts one into a relationship with God.

Legalism is the unlawful use of the law, the illegal use of it. In 1 Timothy chapter 1 we have these words to help clarify legalism: "Now the purpose of the commandment (any commandment of God) is love from a pure heart, from a good conscience and from sincere faith, from which some, having strayed, have turned aside to idle talk, desiring to be teachers of the law, understanding neither what they say nor the things which they affirm." (Remember these words when we get to the first chapter of Galatians.) The way to turn aside from love and faith is to teach and try to live by the law. They are contrary to each other. Legalist teachers do not understand the purpose of the commandments of God, which is to show us that love and faith are the goal of God and the gospel.

Then Paul writes, "But we know that the law is good if one uses it lawfully." We must be clear about this: there is nothing wrong with the law. The problem with the law is *us!* We cannot keep the law, and therefore, we will live under the curse, unless we live by grace. The problem we have is the wrong use of the law. The law is good if one uses it lawfully. "Knowing this, that the law is not made for a righteous person, but for the lawless..." and then he lists the most horrible sinners in the world. When we place our faith in Christ, we are declared righteous by God. We are righteous as far as God is concerned. The law is not for the righteous. That's what he says. All these sins listed are *contrary to sound doctrine*, and sound doctrine is *according to the glorious gospel of the blessed God*. It is the gospel believed that produces righteous living, not the law. According to Romans 7 the law reveals and revives sin; it does not remove sin. Only the grace of God can do that. To live the Christian life, we only need the grace revealed in the gospel.

Paul marveled that the Galatians had so quickly and easily turned away from Him who had called them in the grace of Christ to a different gospel. To pervert the gospel, we can do one of two things: we can either take away from it or add to it. We take away from it by denying that it produces righteous living; it does not necessarily produce godliness. That is a denial of sanctification that the gospel naturally produces. But to add to it, one simply has to say, "Christ is good but not enough." And so we add something to it. The cross is necessary but not sufficient. These legalists say that Christ is first base, but second and third must be added to it to get you home. And those other bases are things like water baptism, keeping the Sabbath, good works, etc.

Actually, Christ is the home run. If you have Him, you score eternal life. You need nothing else. If you add anything to Him, you pervert and destroy the gospel. Paul says that people who do this should be accursed from God. Pretty strong language.

Paul is teaching how to live the Christian life in Galatians, and to live it we must first establish how we were saved in the first place, because how we were saved is how we must live, and that is by grace. So Paul continues in Galatians 2:16: "Knowing that a man is not justified by works of the law, but by faith in Jesus Christ, even we have believed in Christ Jesus, that we might be justified by faith in Christ and not by works of the law; for by the works of the law no flesh shall be justified." And then in Galatians 2:20 he declares that he lives by the faith of the Son of God. The Christian life is to be lived by faith, not by the law. How it commences is how it continues. Nothing we get from God comes by doing the law: "Did you receive the Spirit by the works of the law, or by the hearing of faith? He who supplies the Spirit to you and works miracles among you, does He do it by the works of the law or by the hearing of faith?" These rhetorical questions have an obvious answer. We get everything from God by the hearing of faith, not by the works of the law.

Galatians is the ringing of the Liberty Bell for the Christian. In 5:1–4 Paul uses the strongest possible language to kill legalism in this church: "Stand fast therefore in the liberty by which Christ has made us free, and do not be entangled again with the yoke of bondage." The context clearly shows the liberty is from the law of God, which is that yoke of bondage. "Indeed I, Paul, say to you that if you become circumcised, Christ will profit you nothing." If you try to add any-thing to Christ (baptism, tongues, you name it), then Christ is no benefit to you whatsoever. If you do anything, like be circumcised to be right with God, you are a debtor to keep the whole law.

If you're going to live by the law, you have to live by the whole law; you can't pick and choose which law you will add to the gos-pel. You say the Sabbath, water baptism, tongues, or whatever? Who gives you the right to select which law people are required to obey to be right with God? If you take one, you must take them all. Have you counted the number of laws in the Bible? If you *attempt to be justified by law, you have fallen from grace.* You have fallen from the realm and teaching of grace to the kingdom of law, and you are estranged and separated from Christ. These are some of the most powerful words in the Bible. Circumcision is simply a synecdoche (a figure of speech in which a part is used for the whole) for all the law, any law. If you add anything to the gospel of Christ, you cannot be a Christian or live the Christian life.

When we were lost, we thought we could be right with God by works of the law. Do good and God will receive you. Then the Holy Spirit and the word show us that we are not good and all our righ-teousness is as filthy rags (Isa. 64:6). We cry for mercy: "Have mercy on me, a sinner!" God has mercy and blots out all your sins against Him, and His grace places you into an eternal relationship of favor and blessing, as if you had never sinned. You leave the realm of law and enter the kingdom of grace. And God never changes His mind about that.

You are justified in the sight of God apart from the works of the law. But we must be careful and never think we must live the same way we did before we got saved. Think we will only grow as we try hard to keep the laws of the Bible and the church, that we are accepted by God (and others) only as we perform the rituals and obey the law. This is the first and most formidable foe of the believer.

It is easy to move from being the prodigal son returned home to the elder brother standing outside the father's house critical of the father's mercy on the saved son. In that story the whole scene closes with the elder son outside of the house, critical and complaining. He had placed himself, his brother, and even his father, under the law: Dad wasn't doing what was right.

We cannot walk with God or live with His children if we live by the law, any law, even the law of God. That will lead to anger, judging, condemning, despising one another, and separation. Legalism is the killer of all relationships.

Legalism is trying to earn or maintain a relationship (with God or with anybody else) by obeying certain rules and laws, making others earn a relationship with you. It is *living by the law* and thinking you are good (or someone else is good) simply because you obey a certain code of conduct. It is gaining and maintaining a right standing with someone based on performance. If you do not obey the law (please the other person), you are condemned and the relationship is severed, to some degree or other. If you do, everything's fine. You get along well, if you meet the minimum requirements laid down by the law. Legalism is guided by a list of dos and don'ts, oughts and shoulds. It throws mercy and grace out the window because the other person has not measured up.

I remember the day this happened to me as a believer. I was a pastor in seminary, and I happened to take a Christian ethics course by Dr. Doug Ezell. It took every bit of a four-hour semester course to purge every bit of legalism from my heart. He hammered it four hours a week—relentlessly. The whole class was angry most of the time because we were fighting for our rules to live by, God's rules to live by. The verbal sparring that took place attracted crowds in the hallways. (I found out that he did this every semester. He was a very popular professor at SWBTS.) And he was a veritable Rocky Balboa. Refusing to be knocked down, he kept coming at us with the truth. He was a surgeon, determined to cut all the cancer of legalism out of our brains. He was very good at what he did.

I discovered in those formative years that Christian ethics is *the fruit of the Spirit* (Gal. 5:22–23). All that God requires of me is love, joy, and peace. And that boils down to love. All the law and the prophets is summed up in that word—love. Everything God requires of us is to love. Everything God requires of us is produced in us by the Spirit. It is His fruit.

The gospel is the Magna Charta, the Emancipation Proclamation, to the Christian; and the power of the Holy Spirit is the liberating force of God come to set the captive free. Everything God requires of us (yes, even that which the law of God requires) is produced in us by the Holy Spirit, and that is love.

Legalism is the wrong use of the law. This is the killer. People use the law in ways it was never intended, to do things it cannot do, and it murders their joy, their relationships, and their soul. *Most marriages fail because of legalism.* At the wedding one person spouts his or her vows, promises of what he or she will do. The vows are totally unconditional. The marriage is to picture Christ's relationship to the church, a relationship of unconditional love and commitment. Then in the marriage we are always bringing up what the other is doing wrong. Each gives unconditional vows at the wedding and then enters the marriage full of expectations of what the other is supposed to do. We put our beloved spouses under the law and punish them with withdrawals and other such things. That is legalism. It is placing the most important person in our lives under the law and then judging them when they do not live up to it. This kills a relationship and produces judgment and condemnation instead of love and mercy.

"What if you're married to a jerk?" Be careful whom you marry and to whom you speak vows. "For better or for worse" are the most serious words you will ever speak. Counseling may be needed to fix things from time to time. Love doesn't overlook and enable serious character flaws. Both spouses must be committed to fix things.

We do this with the *children* when we are angry and/or abusive to them for not obeying the laws of the family (house rules). The disciplining of children should always be done in love. Children must never think they have to earn your love or acceptance. Earning acceptance is hard-core legalism. Respect is earned, but love is unconditional. Love keeps no record of wrongs (1 Cor. 13:4–8). Love forgives. Loves sets the other person free. Living under the law is the opposite of living under love. Law and grace are opposites; they never live in the same house.

When my oldest daughter was about fourteen, she grew increasingly quiet and withdrawn. One mealtime she asked to be excused, and so she went to her room. I went to her and asked what was wrong. She cried as she told me something she did that she was ashamed of. I asked her why she didn't say anything at the "evening meal." At our evening meal the four girls could confess anything, and there would be no consequences for whatever they had done. She told me it wasn't about the consequences but that she was afraid if I found out what she had done I wouldn't love me anymore. I set her straight and told her, "Honey, you could never ever do anything to make me stop loving you. If you murdered someone, I'd be the first one to the jail, bringing you food and cigarettes!" (She has never smoked.) When she was composed, I gathered the other three girls into the living room and made it clear to them all that they could never do anything to make me stop loving them.

God is the same way with His children. His love is everlasting, and that means we didn't do anything to make Him start loving us, therefore we can't do anything to make Him stop loving us. (See Romans 5:8.) He doesn't love us because of what we do; He loves us because of who He is. *God is love.* It is that unconditional love that we as Christians live in. We live the Christian life by grace and faith in that love.

Legalism kills *churches*. Much church multiplication has been done by church splits. Churches are known for their fighting, divisions and power struggles. These things come from living under the law. They are products of the flesh and the flesh always works in conjunction with the law. Others don't measure up and we separate ourselves from them. We disagree and divide instead of loving each other. Differences don't divide; legalism divides.

A simple illustration can help us define legalism. The esteemed head of the missions department at Southwestern Baptist Theological Seminary, Dr. Cal Guy, spoke only these profound words at a chapel service to thousands of theological students: "My first point is, billions of people are dying and going to hell, and many of you do not give a damn. My second point is, you are more bothered that I used the word damn than you are that billions are lost and on their way to hell." He sat down and left us to soak in that truth. That is legalism!

The difference between legalism and discipleship is attitude and motivation. The legalist and disciple may be doing the same things, but the person under the law is doing it because he *must*, not necessarily because he *wants* to. Legalism comes from an external law; discipleship is an internal attitude and motivation. The law is written on his heart. "*I will write My laws on their heart,*" God says. When He does that, you do what you do because it is *in* you. You want to do it.

You are deceived if you think that you can relate to God by grace and others by law. Jesus said, "Judge not, that you be not judged. For with what judgment you judge, you will be judged" (Matt. 7:1–2). God *will treat you exactly the way you treat others.* If you do not forgive others, God will not forgive you. "For if you forgive men their trespasses, your heavenly Father will also forgive you. But if you do not forgive men their trespasses, neither will your Father forgive your trespasses. So, My heavenly Father also will do to you if each of you, from his heart, does not forgive his brother his trespasses" (Matt. 6:14–15, 18:21–35).

We (automatically, without even knowing it) put others and ourselves under the law when we judge and condemn others. We put ourselves back under law to God when we put others under the law to us. Our responsibility is not to judge others; it is to love them, to live in peace with them, and rejoice with them; against such there is no law (Gal 5:22–23). *If you really want to be set free, set others free. You set others free, and God will set you free.*

We should pray that God would create a culture of grace and love in every church and in every Christian, that we may walk in freedom and transparency, with no hypocrisy, where everyone can be themselves, where sin is not condoned, but neither is the sinner condemned. The church should be totally free from the illegal use of the law, a place where mercy, forgiveness, and grace reign. In Christ we are free to love God and others, even as Christ has loved us. The antidote to the legalism is the liberty of love. Just love one another. Be at peace with one another. Legalism divides people, even Christian people. Love reconciles and brings people together. You can't live with God if you can't live with others in peace and love, and you can't do that if you put others under the law. To live the Christian life, we must live in love and not under the law. Let people go. Set them free. Love them. No matter what.

HOW TO LIVE THE CHRISTIAN LIFE

How to Get Along with Everybody All the Time

> *Let nothing be done through strife or pride; but in*
> *lowliness of mind let each esteem others better than*
> *themselves. Be like Jesus; He humbled himself.*
> —Philippians 2:2–9

> *Whoever therefore shall humble himself as this little child,*
> *the same is the greatest in the kingdom of heaven.*
> —Matthew 18:1–4

If I were to ask you to give me one word that would sum up everything needed to get along with everybody all the time, what would it be? There is such a word, and if this was part of our character, we could get along with everybody all the time. It is the word *humble. Humility is the key to harmony*. But humbling ourselves is the hardest thing for us to do. It takes the grace of God to be humble. We cannot do this on our own because we are in love with ourselves more than anybody else. We hate to get down. We hate to get dirty.

The word *humility* comes from the word *humas*, which means dirt. Humans were made from dirt. From dirt we came, and to dirt we shall return. The earth is beneath us. To be humble means to get low, to lower ourselves. In Asian cultures, when people meet and greet, they bow. They humble themselves before another. It's a way of showing respect and honor, getting lower than others.

We walk on dirt. That's where the rub comes in. Humility is the key to getting along with others, but if you act like dirt, people will walk on you, and nobody wants to be walked on. We don't want to be treated like a doormat. People walk on doormats, and the dirt from other people's shoes gets on doormats.

And God expects us to do this? To humble ourselves? Yes! The greatest and most valuable thing in the world is harmony. It must be because there is so little of it. God honors this virtue more than all others. In fact, the inspired three-word summary of the life and death of Jesus Christ is "He humbled Himself." The word of God continually extols this character trait. It is the thing that carries the greatest promises to us from God, and by humility we gain the greatest rewards. "Humble yourselves before the mighty hand of God that He may exalt you in due time" (1 Pet. 5:6). "God resists the proud but gives grace to the humble" (James 4:6).

Of course, all this humility stuff flies in the face of the current culture of self-esteem where we are taught to esteem ourselves and love ourselves above all others. But God's take on this is quite different. "Whoever exalts himself will be humbled, and he who humbles himself will be exalted" (Luke 14:11). With God the way up is down. We get low, and He lifts us up.

Back to our topic. *Harmony always comes from humility.* The moment pride enters the door, strife comes in with it. They are Siamese twins. You can't have one without the other. No humility, no harmony. That's why Paul, when he urges the believers in Philippi to live in harmony, writes, "Let nothing be done through strife and don't let pride be your guide, but in lowliness of mind. (Think lowly of yourself. If you knew yourself like God knows you, you would.) Let each esteem others better than themselves. Consider others more valuable than yourself. Consider their needs more important than yours. Look not on your own things, but also on the things of others."

Note the word *others* in this text is used twice (v. 3–4). Jesus came for others. He didn't consider His exalted position in heaven as the Son of God something to be held on to for Himself. Instead, He emptied Himself of all His honor and highness and came to earth as a baby. Remember, a human body is made of dirt. God became a man! Why would He do such a thing? For others. He did everything He did for others. He came for others. He lived for others. He served others. He healed others. He fed others. He delivered others. He even died for others. They could have put a sign over His blessed head on that cross that said "*Others,*" and it would fit perfectly. He even lives right now as our High Priest, interceding for others. He is one day coming back for others.

It should not surprise us that our God calls us to do what He has always done. Think of others. Live for others. Stop thinking only of yourself. Lack of humility is the reason for the disharmony in your life.

Now I don't mean that if you humble yourself, people will always get along with you! We are to by all means possible live in peace with others, but that doesn't mean they will live in peace and get along with us. Jesus got along with everybody all the time, but everybody didn't get along with Him. Oh no! They crucified Him! Humility gets walked on...by men. But remember, God exalts the humble, in His own time.

God wants us thinking like Jesus: "Let this mind be in you which was also in Christ Jesus." Think the way Jesus thought. How did He think? "He humbled Himself." But as a result of that, look what God did: "Wherefore God also has highly exalted Him and given Him a name which is above every name." What God did for Jesus (exalt Him because of His humility) He will in do for us. He will richly reward the humble. Trust Him. Humility is great because it requires us to trust God.

In Matthew 18:1–4 Jesus teaches on the greatness of humility. Not only can we not get along with others without humbling ourselves, we cannot get along with God without it. To get along with the most important person in the universe, the judge of every living human, who has the power to destroy both body and soul in hell, we must humble ourselves. This is the way to live the Christian life, the only way to live the Christian life.

There is nothing wrong with the question the disciples asked Jesus: "Who is the greatest in the kingdom of heaven?" We know from Jesus's response that they were not talking about certain people here. "Jesus, is John greater than Peter?" They are asking what type of person is the greatest in the kingdom of heaven. We know this from Jesus's answer to their question. He places a little child in front of them and says this is the type of person who is greatest with the king of heaven.

There is nothing wrong with wanting to be great for God. Everyone should want to be great for the name of Jesus. Let my name perish; but let His glorious name, that name which is above every name, be exalted. Exalted by the way I live and talk. We should want to do great things for God. And what could be greater than to live in humility like He did when He was among us? And to prefer others above yourself? And to serve others? That's humility, and that is greatness.

Jesus teaches us here that greatness comes from humility. More than that, He teaches that entrance into the kingdom is through the straight, narrow, and low gate of humility. We can't even enter the kingdom of heaven without becoming as humble as a little child.

There are several things about babies that show humility. They *don't know anything*. They don't know math, or even their own hand. It's funny to see a baby first discover his hand. That look is precious. Little ones *can't do anything*. They can't cook or walk or drive a car. They basically can't do anything to help themselves. They are pretty much helpless. Lastly, they *don't have anything*. They are born naked. They came into the world with nothing. A newborn prince owns nothing. The castle he lives in is not his. The clothes he wears are not his. He owns nothing.

Now, we come into the kingdom just like that. We don't know anything…but what God tells us. We know a lot, but none of it is true. We can only trust what God tells us. Is that the way you are? A newborn Christian cannot do anything. He may have many talents, but they are no good for the kingdom of God unless He sanctifies and anoints them. His talents are useless as far and the kingdom of God is concerned. And he doesn't own anything. God has given him everything he has—on loan. God is the maker and owner of all things. The new believer puts all his assets to the disposal of the Savior who became poor that we might be made rich. In fact, to get into the kingdom of God, we ask the same thing Saul asked when he met Jesus: "Lord, what would you have me to do?" (Acts 9:6). My agenda doesn't matter anymore. "I have suffered the loss of all things that I might gain Christ," Paul said in Philippians 3:7–8.

If we want to live the Christian life, we must live humbly. We must humble ourselves, before God and others. Think first of others. Seek peace. We must admit when we are wrong. Take the low road. Do this and you will get along with everybody all the time. Sure, there is more to it, but this is the entrance into the kingdom, and this is how we live the greatest life. Humble yourself. You don't want God to humble you.

Husbands and wives need to remember this: "I'm not going to let him walk all over me!" Why? They walked on Jesus. Are you better than Jesus? To keep from living as doormats, we should seek to solve the differences. Talk about the problem. But in the end, to end all conflict, humble yourself. In the long run you'll be glad you did. "I dwell in the high and holy place with him who has a contrite and humble spirit, to revive the spirit of the humble" (Isa. 57:15).

HOW TO LIVE THE
CHRISTIAN LIFE

The Way We Treat Others Is the Way We Treat Christ

Whoever receives one little child like this in My name receives Me.
—Matthew 18:5

How to get along with others all the time is exactly what this amazing chapter from the mouth of Jesus is all about. And who does not want to get along with others?

Before anything else we must get along with God (v. 1–4). *Humility is the key to a relationship with God,* and everybody else for that matter. "Whoever humbles himself as this little child is the greatest in the kingdom of heaven." And humility is no less the major ingredient to getting along with others. In the beginning of the "getting along with others" section of scripture, which actually goes through the rest of Matthew 18 Jesus states an amazing truth that will help more than anything else. *We are to treat other believers in Christ the way we would treat Christ.* And make no mistake about it, He is talking about Christians here: Christians treating other Christians like they would treat Christ Himself. When He talks about receiving one little child, He has already identified in verse 3 who the little children are He is talking about. This is the way to get along with other church members. Is this not important? It is of paramount importance to the church and the world. Our peace in the family of

God and our witness in the world depend on this. We must be one if they are to know that Jesus is the Savior.

Keep in mind that the key to getting along with others all the time is not what others do to you or say about you. Jesus said, "Offenses must come" (Matt. 18:7). People are going to treat you badly. (Leave them to God. Vengeance is His. He will repay.) You will be offended. You will be sinned against. People are going to do you wrong. They are going to talk bad about you and hurt you. The key to getting along with others is how *you* treat them, not how they treat you. You can't keep them from wronging you, but you can keep from wronging them. Your response to their misbehavior is your responsibility. How you respond to the abuses of others is up to you. How you treat those who offend you is your choice.

There are four main degrees of how we should treat others according to the Scriptures.

1. *The Law.* If you lived according to the law of God, you would never hurt or wrong anyone. "Love does no harm to a neighbor; therefore, love is the fulfillment of the law" (Rom. 13:10). If you loved your neighbor, you would not steal from him, bear false witness against him, or murder him. If you refrained from hurting anybody, you would basically be loving them and obeying the law. If church people would just do this, how great the church's reputation in the community would be. Jesus kept His Father's law; He never hurt anybody.

2. *The Golden Rule*, which says to *do unto others as you would have them do unto you* (Matt. 7:12). Note this is positive and a step up from the law. Jesus brought a whole new dimension to what is required of us. Not only do no harm but do good. If your neighbor is hungry, feed him; naked, clothe him; lonely, visit him. Do good to him because you want him to do good to you. Treat others the way you would like them to treat you. Do you want them to gossip about you? Then don't gossip about them. This is not just don't hurt

anybody, it's help them. Do good to them. This is what Jesus did. "He went about doing good" (Acts 10:38).

3. *Treat others the way Christ has treated you.* How is that? With grace and love and patience and understanding and mercy and compassion. Treat others that way. In Romans 15:7 we have this: "Receive one another, just as Christ has received us, to the glory of God." Receiving each other as you have been received by Christ is to the glory of God. How has Christ received you? Like the father received the prodigal son in Luke 15. And like the shepherd received the lost sheep. He searched for it until he found it and brought it back into the fold (Matt. 18:12–14). These two illustrations are insightful and informative because they speak of receiving others who have not been right. These are sometime the hardest to receive.

4. *How you treat others is how you treat Christ.* Treating others the way you would treat Christ is the highest level of getting along with others. We are to receive one another the way we would receive Jesus Christ. "Whoever receives one little child in My name receives Me." If you receive another believer, you receive Christ. A group of men at a renowned historical society assembly were discussing who from history they would most like to see walk through the door. One said Alexander the Great, another Christopher Columbus, another Thomas Edison, still another George Washington. But the last man said, "If any of those men walked in, we would all stand to honor such an esteemed person. But if the one I am going to mention walked through that door, we would all get on our faces and worship. I'd like to see Jesus Christ walk through that door." Now I'm not suggesting we all hit the floor when we meet another Christian, but it does say something of how we should treat another believer, with honor and respect. He is after all a prince and a child of God.

One of the most awesome revelations I have ever received is that the way we treat another believer is the way we treat Christ, a fact borne out by a ton of scriptures. When Jesus talked about receiving *one little child*, He is talking about another Christian. We are to receive another believer as we would receive Christ.

Why would you *not* do that? Three possible reasons: (1) You think you are better than they are. You consider yourself more important than that other believer. You're too important to be treating him like you'd treat Jesus. But Christ didn't think like this. And the Bible says, "In lowliness of mind let each esteem others better than himself" (Phil. 2:3–4). If you break one commandment, you are guilty of them all (James 2:10). Isaiah the prophet saw the Lord in His holiness and called himself an unclean man with unclean lips. (2) You think they are not worthy of you treating them like Jesus. Well, you need to remember how that prodigal son was treated by his father, who represented God in that story (Luke 15). That son was received with delight by that father and with disdain by the elder brother. Why disdain? Because he thought his younger brother didn't deserve to be treated so well, received with such delight and celebration. And after all, he had never even had a goat given to him by his dad! That older son was last seen standing outside the father's house. He did not and would not receive his undeserving brother as his father had. What a lesson for us!

The way we treat one another is not only noticed by Christ, it is important to Him. Look at verse 10, then verses 11–14: "Take heed that you do not despise one of these little ones, for I say to you that in heaven their angels always see the face of My Father who is in heaven." The "their angels" comment means each believer has a guardian angel and that angel is looking at the face of God. When we don't receive another believer, the very countenance of God changes toward us. A mighty angel sees it and goes into action against us (v. 6–7). "For the Son of Man has come to save that which is lost. If a man has a 100 sheep and one of them goes astray, does he not leave the 99 and go to the mountains to seek the one that is straying?" That's how Jesus sees the child who is straying. How do you see him?

Another thing (3) that will keep you from getting along with another Christian is what you hear from other people about that person. Others can sour your feelings toward someone, and you don't even know if a word of what they say is true or not! And even if the things others say are true, you should still treat that brother as though he were Christ. One church member told me that a certain lady whose family had been coming to our church was bragging on me like I was the best thing that ever happened to our county. "Best preacher I've ever heard!" Her family had missed a couple of weeks, and he ran into her and asked where they'd been. The woman had talked to somebody else and said she couldn't come back to hear me preach solely because of what this other person said about me! What changed? What another person had told her. And she never talked to me to see if any of it was true!

One lady in this town that I don't remember ever even meeting before came up to me and said, "I need to ask you to forgive me." I said I surely would but wondered why I needed to. She told me she had heard a bunch of bad things about me, believed them, and had only recently found out they were not true. So you can take up an offense against others and from that moment on you can't get along with them. Careful that you do not take up an offense against someone because someone else told you a bunch of stuff and poured acid on your soul toward that other person. From that moment on, you can't get along with that other person because of what you have heard. Don't let others embitter your soul toward another.

Never forget this: *the works of the flesh are anger, bitterness, gossip, backbiting, malice while the fruit of the Spirit is love and peace, patience, and kindness.* These things are obvious. But multitudes don't know the difference simply because the gossip comes to them from a friend. One deacon left the church, and when I went to see him, he told me it was because his brother-in-law left the church. When I asked him why the brother-in-law left the church, he said he didn't know, but if he left there must be something wrong! And this man was a deacon! Never hold a grudge against anyone. Let it go! Give it to God. Here's why.

The way you treat a fellow believer in Christ is the way you treat Christ. He takes your treatment of others personally. Saul was treating Christians very badly, persecuting them to prison and to death. But when Christ arrested him, He asked him, "Saul, Saul, why do you persecute Me?" Saul asked Him who He was and He answered, "*I am Jesus.*" Saul had not been persecuting Jesus; he had been persecuting the church. But Jesus saw it as the same. What we do to others we do to Jesus. That's how He sees it, and that's how it is.

In Matthew 25:37–40 and 44–46 we have Jesus saying that people were being sent to hell because He had been thirsty and they didn't so much as give Him a drink; hungry and they didn't feed Him. They asked Him when they saw Him thirsty and hungry, and He said to them, "Inasmuch as you did not do it to one of the least of these My brethren, you did not do it to Me." *The way you treat others is the way you treat Jesus.*

HOW TO LIVE THE
CHRISTIAN LIFE

What to Do When Others Wrong You

Moreover, if you brother sins against you...
—Matthew 18:15–35

T he first fourteen verses of this amazing chapter on personal relation-ships is about making sure you don't sin against others. Don't start any-thing. The key to getting along with others is getting along with God. For that it takes humility. Man is a very humble being; he was made from the dust of the ground. But because of his dignity in creation and his sinful nature that he got from sin, he loves himself more than he loves others and he thinks mostly of himself and his own. In his self-righteous pride he imagines himself his own boss with knowledge, abilities, and possessions that even impress God. So the first thing the Holy Spirit must do is convince him of his sinfulness: "There is none good; no, not one" is the testimony of God. To admit that is to humble yourself.

If in humility you cry out to God for mercy, He will have mercy. And the same thing that gets you into God's kingdom is what makes you great in that kingdom—humility. And it is the only thing that will enable you to get along with everybody all the time. Growing out of that we have Jesus's teachings on the way we treat others. First, the way we treat others is the way we treat Christ. God must show us that, and He does by what Jesus says in verses 5–15: "Whoever receives one of these little ones who believe in Me receives Me" (v. 5–6).

So make sure you don't mistreat others in God's family, and by extension anybody else, for we often don't know who are or will be members of the family. Offending one of them brings horrible judgment in hell. Jesus takes this stuff personally, and He has angels ready to go into action against those who sin against His kids.

But then Jesus pivots from talking about making sure you don't sin against others to what to do when others wrong you (v. 15–35). He begins this section with these words: "Moreover when your brother sins against you..." He takes the rest of the chapter to tell us what to do when that happens: how to get along with people who mistreat you.

I remind you, what He tells us to do in this passage is not easy. It must not be, because most people can't seem to do it. These simple instructions that it seems like anybody could follow take the grace and power of the Holy Spirit to perform. Without grace and the Spirit, we will strike back when others wrong us. We will take vengeance, do the old "eye for an eye" thing, repay them in kind. That only makes matters worse. They talk bad about you; you talk bad about them. They steal from you; you steal from them. They lie about you; you tell a bigger one about them. That's only right, right? Wrong!

We are called to follow Christ's example, "who, when He was reviled, did not revile in return; when He suffered, He did not threaten" (1 Pet. 2:20–25). He not only told us what to do when others sin against us (Matt. 5:38–48), He showed us what to do when others arrested Him, abused Him, falsely accused Him, beat Him unjustly, and nailed Him to a cross. He is the One we follow. Do what Jesus would do. But that takes Jesus's help.

So, before we go any further, we need to ask God to help us do these things. Commit yourself to do them, and then ask God to remind you of your commitment when someone wrongs you.

A word needs to be said about what you do when others do not sin against you, you just don't approve of or like what they did. Or maybe you just are associated with someone who is just hard to get along with. How do you get along with someone who is not necessarily wronging you but they are turned different than you are? They rub you the wrong way. Maybe they don't treat you with the honor and kindness you think they should. Well, differences are not sins, and differences shouldn't divide. Disagreements don't divide. God made us different, and that's okay. The flesh divides. Pride divides. Just because someone disagrees with you or doesn't see things your way, does not mean they are wronging you. What do you do to get along with these people?

Romans 14:1 admonishes us to "receive one who is weak in the faith, but not to disputes over doubtful things." Then in verses 3 and 10 it tells us why: "For God has received him." The next verse tells us, "Who are you to judge another's servant? Why do you judge your brother? Or why do you show contempt for your brother? For we shall all stand before the judgment seat of Christ. So, then each of us shall give an account of himself to God." You don't want to be sitting at the Judge's bench when He comes into the courtroom. We are called to sit in the witness seat, not on the Judge's bench.

The church with the most problems in the New Testament was the one at Corinth. Paul's first letter to them, chapter 13, teaches us to love one another. *Love for one another is the cure for divisions over differences.* You don't have to agree with others to love them.

The remainder of Matthew 18 (v. 15–35) deals with getting along with those who actually *sin* against us, those who actually do us wrong. We are not to think it strange when people mistreat us. "Offenses must come," Jesus said, and they will come. You might think it shouldn't happen, but don't think for a moment that it won't happen, because it will. We are like porcupines on a cold morning: we need each other, but then we needle each other. Christians sin! What a revelation! Much of the teachings in the Bible deal with that very subject: believers sinning against each other. Esau hated Jacob; Joseph's brothers sinned against him; the Exodus generation spent forty years sinning against Moses. Name a judge that wasn't sinned against. Name a king. How about the greatest of kings, David? Name a prophet who wasn't sinned against, or an apostle? Jesus was certainly sinned against. You and I will be wronged, and the closer those who do are to us, the more it hurts.

Verses 15–20 tells us how church members are to deal with (and help!) people who sin against you. We need to help sinners. I mean, church members who sin against you! They need your help. They don't need to keep doing that; and you are the one to help them because you are the one they sinned against. And they may need the help of the church. It has been well said that the Christian army is the only one that shoots its wounded. But instead of that, we are called upon to reconcile with them, to help them make it right and live right. If we don't help them, who will? We are their brothers and sisters, members of the same family, with the same Father.

First, have a *private* meeting (v. 15). Don't talk to others about him: "Go and tell him his fault between you and him alone." That will usually solve most of the relationship problems in the church. But if it doesn't, have a *plural* meeting: "Take with you one or two more." These should be witnesses, not just friends. They should know firsthand that this person has sinned against you. If that doesn't work, have a *public* meeting: "Tell it to the church." If that doesn't work, do what Jesus says here, but throw in a parallel passage that can help. I'm speaking of 1 Corinthians 5:4–12 and Romans 16:17. The whole church is to not fellowship with this person until he repents. The purpose of church discipline is to bring the so-called brother to repentance. Love seeks to do this.

Important things hinge on our obeying these simple and clear instructions (v. 18–20). Unity in the church gives us authority in the Lord to help or release people "Assuredly, I say to you, whatever you bind on earth will be bound in heaven, and whatever you loose on earth will be loosed in heaven." (v. 18) Without dealing with disunity, we will be defeated in spiritual warfare. Harmony is necessary to have our prayers answered "Again I say to you that if two of you agree on earth concerning anything that they ask, it will be done for them by My Father in heaven." (v. 19) And unity brings the special presence of the Lord into the church "For where two or three are gathered together in My name, I am there in the midst of them." (v. 20) The dove of the Spirit doesn't light on troubled waters.

Then Peter brings up the matter of forgiveness (v. 21): "How often shall my brother sin against me, and I forgive him?" Church discipline is one thing, but what about forgiving the person who has sinned against you? Should you just keep forgiving him and letting him keep getting away with it? This deals with our attitude toward the errant brother. The church is to *note and avoid* him. So does that mean we don't have to forgive him? No, it does not. We are to forgive him as long as he needs it.

Some very important lessons are taught in the parable Jesus tells on forgiveness. And never forget, if God can't get along with anybody without forgiveness, then neither can we. Forgiveness must reign in the heart of every believer. If someone sins against you, you must forgive them. Here's why.

1. God requires us to treat others the same way He treats us. "I forgave you all that debt because you begged me. Should you not also have had compassion on your fellow servant, just as I had compassion on you?" (v. 32–33).

2. The way we treat others is how God will treat us. "His master was angry and delivered him to the torturers… So My Heavenly Father also will do to you if each of you, from his heart, does not forgive his brother his trespasses" (v. 34–35). What a sobering truth this is! In Matthew 6:14–15 Jesus said, "If you forgive men their trespasses, your heavenly Father will also forgive you. But if you do not forgive men their trespasses, neither will your Father forgive your trespasses." If you show no mercy toward your brother, you will get no mercy from God. So how do you want God to treat you? With severity or goodness? (Rom. 11:22) You choose the way God treats you by how you treat others. "For judgment is without mercy to the one who shows no mercy" (James 2:13). "Judge not, that you be not judged. For with what judgment you judge, you will be judged; and with the same measure you use, it will be measured back to you" (Matt. 7:1–2).

In conclusion, do you need to confess and ask forgiveness from anyone? Do it and the sooner the better. Or have you been hurt or wronged by someone? Go to God and cast your care upon Him, for He cares for you (1 Pet. 5:7). Then ask God to help you forgive that other person. He will. Jesus paid for all forgiveness at the cross. Our *motive* for forgiving others is the fact that we have been forgiven much. The *measure* of our forgiveness is seven times seventy, but don't keep count. The *manner* of forgiveness is *from the heart.* The *means* is Christ.

HOW TO LIVE THE CHRISTIAN LIFE

Worship and Warfare

Let the high praises of God be in the mouths of the saints and a two-edged sword in their hand.
—Psalm 149:6 and 150

We cannot possibly live the Christian life without both worshiping God and warring against our enemies. Worship brings God into our lives in a very real and powerful way, and with Him we can defeat the spiritual forces of wickedness in our lives. To learn this, we look to Israel's greatest king—David.

Did you notice the connection Psalm 149:6 made between worship and warfare? Worship is not just giving God the glory. If that's all we did when we worship God, that would be enough. He is worthy of our worship. It's the right thing to do. But there's a lot more at stake in praising God in song and music. If you want the devil to flee from you, start praising God. And the best way to do that continually is to let the high praises of God be in our mouths. Praise Him in the sanctuary. Praise Him with all these musical instruments talked about in Psalm 150. Let your home and car be filled with the music from heaven, continually. The spiritual forces of wickedness will not hang around where God is being praised. Deliverance comes through praise. The battles for your life are won in worship.

Let it not surprise us that David, the greatest king Israel ever knew, only did two things. He was only known for two things. One was worship. David was a *worshiper*, perhaps the greatest worshiper ever. He was chosen by God to teach His people to worship. He wrote most of the Hebrew hymnal, the book of Psalms. He invented musical instruments with which to praise God. Read all of Psalms 150 and you will see a man who was given to worshiping God with everything he had, all his body and soul and mind. "Praise Him with the trumpet, the lute and harp, the timbral, the dance, with stringed instruments, flutes, loud cymbals, clashing cymbals. Let everything that has breath praise the Lord." And if you can't play music, "Oh clap your hands, all you people, shout unto God with the voice of triumph" (Ps. 47:7).

Our bodies and voices become musical instruments for the praising of God. All this can be done anywhere, but the primary place encouraged by David was "Praise God in the sanctuary" (Ps. 150:1). And just to make sure we get it, David writes, "Let them praise His name with the dance." This is using all your body and soul to worship God. David not only said to do this, he did it. He danced before God in the middle of the streets of Jerusalem with the whole nation watching.

God made each of to be musical instruments. When He created everything on the earth, things just sort of popped out of the ground. He said, "Let the earth bring forth the living creature...and it was so" (Gen. 1:24). But when it came to man, He didn't do it this way. Every musical instrument makes sounds by either being touched or with breath. We either beat it, or strum it or strike it, or we blow through it. When God made man, He "formed man of the dust of ground, and breathed into his nostrils the breath of life..." (Gen.2:7). He formed man. He knelt down and took His hands and formed man. He touched him. Then He blew into him. He made man a musical instrument for the praise and glory of God. Man was made to praise God by his whole being. This is never more demonstrated nor better done than when we are making music and singing to the Lord.

God had made Lucifer with the ability to play music to worship God, but of course, he blew it and became Satan (Ezek. 28:13). Much of worldly music is demonic. We must be careful. Some of the best the world has to offer can come from the devil himself. God made man to replace the fallen Lucifer as instruments of worship. We were made to worship, complete with musical abilities, which includes music and singing.

Worship was only one thing David was known for. There's another, and they go together. David was a man of war. He was a *warrior* like no other warrior. "Saul has killed his thousands and David his ten thousands" was the number one dance tune on the pop charts back in the day (1 Sam. 18:7). When God chose a man to lead His people, to reign over His people, to teach His people, He chose a man who was both a worshiper and a warrior. We learn so much about how to walk with and work for God from this man.

The first thing we learn is that *he was anointed and filled with the Holy Spirit*. "Then Samuel took the horn of oil and anointed him in the midst of his brothers; and the Spirit of the Lord came upon David from that day forward" (1 Sam. 16:13). This is paramount in the life of every believer. If we are to work for God, we need to be filled with the Spirit. If we are to war against the enemies of our souls, we must be anointed by the Spirit. If we are to worship God, it is necessary to be filled with the Holy Spirit. Right after Paul writes, "Be filled with the Spirit," he says, "Speaking to one another in psalms and hymns and spiritual songs, singing and making melody in your heart to the Lord" (Eph. 5:18–19). The Spirit-filled saint is a song-filled saint. And the melody is cast right into heaven—live!

Martin Luther said, "Next to the word of God, music deserves the highest praise." He is the Reformer who wrote one of the greatest hymns of all time: "A Mighty Fortress Is Our God." The message of God carried in a melody may be the most powerful weapon we have in our arsenal.

We all need this if we are going to reign with Christ on this earth as David did. He begins in the pasture with the sheep, worshiping God. David was a worshiper and a warrior even back then. Even before he faced Goliath and led Israel in battle to defeat all their enemies, he had to face lions and bears out in the wild when he was taking care of his father's sheep. Can't you see David out there, maybe at night with the sheep in the makeshift corral and David sitting by the campfire playing his homemade harp (guitar), making up songs and dancing like the soldier on *Dances with Wolves* after he learned the ways of the Indians?

When God rejected King Saul, He told Samuel, the prophet, that He had found a man to replace him: "A man after My own heart," He said. How'd He know that? He'd watched him out there singing and playing and dancing. He's watching you too. He knows if you have a heart after Him by the way you worship. What God had found was a boy out under the stars keeping watch over his father's flocks by night.

God put His Spirit upon a worshiper. When David comes to the palace, it is as a musician and a worshiper. We know his slingshot was a weapon, but watch this. He goes to do spiritual warfare, not with his sling but with his harp. Saul is in a dark place, brought there by the judgment of God for his disobedience. He is demonized. We might be surprised how much of our emotional darkness and defeat is the result of demons that hold us captive in their darkness. Our souls are down, discouraged, depressed. Our bodies are sick, and our minds are tormented with fears and worries and a spirit of rejection. There is a cure. Watch what David does.

The story continues in 1 Samuel 16:14–23. There is Saul tormented by a demon. We know there are demon spirits that hold us in dark dungeons of defeat and discouragement. We know we feel that way, but many times we don't know it is the devil who is doing that to us. Now notice what David does to drive out the evil spirit. Read it in verse 23: "David would take his harp and play it with his hand. Then Saul would become refreshed and well, and the distressing spirit would depart from him."

Worship is a mighty weapon against the spiritual forces of wickedness that torment us and defeat us. This is what happens when the saints in the sanctuary worship with praise music to the Lord. *We worship and war when we sing with music to the Lord.* So let's do it. Regularly. Often. When the praises go up, the Spirit comes down. And when the Spirit comes down, evil spirits depart.

This is epically portrayed for us in 2 Chronicles 20:20–22. Three enemy armies had come against Judah. King Jehoshaphat called for a national prayer meeting. In the midst of that, a prophet spoke and gave the people renewed faith in God their deliverer. In the battle strategy, they sent out first, not the minuscule army of Judah but the choir. They sent out the choir! "He appointed those who should sing to the Lord, and who should praise (This is musical instruments; see Psalm 150) the beauty of holiness, as they went out before the army, singing, 'Praise the Lord, for His mercy endures forever.' Now when they began to sing and to praise, the Lord set ambushes against the people of Ammon, Moab, and Mouth Seir, when had come against Judah; and they were defeated." Worship and warfare go together. God has married them, and they will not ever be divorced.

The will of God is done perfectly in heaven. Heaven is…heaven! There is no devil in heaven. And what is going on there? Continual praise to God. Seraphim cease not to cry continually, "*Holy, Holy, Holy, is the Lord God Almighty*" (Isa. 6). And what is going on there right now and what is it we will be doing in heaven forever? Singing praises to God with musical instruments. This is what is happening in heaven: "And they sang a new song, saying: 'You are worthy to take the scroll, and to open its seals; for You were slain and have redeemed us to God by Your blood out of every tribe and tongue and people and nation, and have made us kings and priests to our God; and we shall reign on the earth'" (Rev. 5:9–10).

Some spiritual dullards want to excuse their lack of heartfelt and body-expressed worship by saying things like this: "Well, if God was doing something in my life, then I would worship Him like the Bible says." One man told me that he wouldn't mind the worship service going long if God were doing something. I asked him what else would God need to do to move in worship? He has sent His Son to die on the cross for our sorry souls. What else would it take to worship Him from now on? God has already done something *big*. He has died on a cross for our sins and risen from the dead to save from hell. That is the very theme of the worship in heaven. And it should be the theme of our lives.

If you are feeling down, it may be that a distressing spirit is doing this to you. Let the music play. Call David in to play. Listen to some worship music. Go to the sanctuary. Go to church and worship God.

HOW TO LIVE THE CHRISTIAN LIFE

Pray

If you abide in Me and My words abide in you, you will ask what you desire and it will be done for you.

—John 15:7

Pray without ceasing.

—1 Thessalonians 5:17

To live the Christian life, we have to pray. We began it by praying. "Whoever calls on the name of the Lord will be saved." (Rom. 10:13). Prayer is to our souls what breathing is to our bodies. We cannot walk with God without prayer. Prayer is not talking to God; it is talking with God. Communion with the Holy Spirit is absolutely essential to living the Christian life. So we must learn how to do it, and do it right.

We want to learn how to pray so we can pray! We won't pray if we don't learn how. We can learn how without praying, but we can't pray unless we learn how, at least not in any effective way. Prayer is the most important thing we can do. It must be because Jesus did so much of it. "Now in the morning, having risen a long while before daylight, He went out and departed to a solitary place; and there He prayed" (Mark. 1:35).

Prayer is communion with God, and can anything be more important than that? The most important thing you could ever learn is how to pray. John taught his disciples how to pray and so did Jesus (Luke 11:1–13). We've got to learn to pray. Why?

1. So many don't know how (Luke 11:1–2).

    This is an obvious fact. They admit it. One night Jesus said to His disciples, "Could you not tarry with Me one hour" (Mark14:37–28). Most don't pray one hour a year! Fact is, many don't pray much because they don't know how. If you don't know how, you need to learn.

2. Jesus taught how to pray (Luke11:2–8).

    He taught them "to pray" by His example, then He taught them how to pray by His words. If the Lord teaches something in His word, then His followers ought to learn what He teaches.

3. God commands us to pray (Luke11:9).

    "Ask, seek and knock" are imperatives. "Then He spoke a parable to them that men always ought to pray and not lose heart" (Luke18:1). God commands us to do the very best thing we could ever do for ourselves. To disobey the command to pray is not only to disobey God, it keeps us from the fount of all blessings.

4. Jesus gave such precious and powerful promises concerning prayer (Luke11:9, Mark11:24–25).

    "And I say to you, ask, and it will be given to you; seek, and you will find; knock, and it will be opened to you. For everyone who asks receives, and he who seeks finds, and to him who knocks it will be opened." Powerful words! Then we have these: "Have faith in God. Therefore, I say to you, whatever things you ask when you pray, believe that you receive them, and you will have them." We need to believe these promises and pray!

5. Every descent of the Holy Spirit in the Bible and in church history upon His people has been preceded by prayer (Luke 11:13, 3:21–22; Acts 1–2). We call these revivals. When

God ordains to bless His people, He first sets them to praying. This world needs revival more than anything else. This does not come without prayer.

6. Jesus said, "My house shall be called a house of prayer" (Mark 11:17).

Today the house of God could be called a house of preaching, a house of entertainment, a house of fellowship, a house of games, a house of Bible study. But Jesus called it a house of prayer. When we cease to pray, we cease to be the house of God. When we cease to be the house of prayer, we cease to be anything but another secular organization.

7. God does nothing except by His Holy Spirit, and He gives Him only in answer to prayer (Luke11:13, James 4:2, Ezek. 36:36–37). Prayer is the means by which the Holy Spirit comes upon people and does His mighty work. If in our conscious weakness we call upon Him, He becomes our strength. All of this means that prayer is the most important thing we can do. Prayer should have the priority in our lives, families, and church.

8. Our testimony (and message) depends upon our prayers (Ezek. 36:38).

Imagine a closed universe consisting only of what is in the room you are in. You are a believer in God, and the only other person in the room is an atheist. He believes that only what he can detect with his senses and equipment is what exists. You tell him that there is a God who is invisible. He doesn't believe it. (This is where most witnessing stops.) But then the clock on the wall in the room stops. He proceeds to fix it, but cannot. You tell him you will pray that God will fix the clock. He laughs; but then stops laughing when, in answer to your prayer, the clock starts ticking again. Now he is ready to listen to what you have to say about God.

9. Ask yourself, "How successful is my prayer life?"

How many answers to prayer are you getting? I mean, pinpoint answers that could only be God doing it in answer to your prayer. If you have been on the same road for twenty years and haven't arrived at your destination, maybe you're on the wrong road. If you have been praying for as long as you've been a Christian and your prayer life is not what it should be, maybe you need to do something different. Maybe you need to learn how to pray.

Let us enroll in His school of prayer and be good students. Our grade will be the answers to the prayers we pray. We have got to learn how to pray.

Okay, so how do we pray? Teach me. We learn from Jesus this most important truth: as His word abides in us, we can ask what we want and God will do it. When we learn the word, we should pray the word. God will answer His word. His word will not return to Him empty. It will accomplish what He sent it out to accomplish—if we return it to Him in prayer.

"Now this is the confidence that we have in Him, that if we ask anything according to His will, He hears us. And if we know that He hears us, whatever we ask, we know that we have the petitions that we have asked of Him" (1 John 5:14–15). We know God's will by knowing God's word. His word is His will. Pray the word. That's the most powerful praying there is because it is sure to get an answer.

The second greatest lesson in the school of prayer is perseverance. Jesus gives this important picture of prayer in Luke 11:5–8. A man needs food for a traveling friend, so he goes to a neighbor for help. The neighbor is not a good neighbor; he won't give him any food. But then he finally does. Why? Not because he is his neighbor but "because of his persistence." Another place Jesus teaches this is in Luke 18:1–8 where it says, "Men always ought to pray and not to lose heart." A widow can't get justice from an unmerciful judge, but he finally said, "Though I do not fear God nor regard man, yet because this widow troubles me I will avenge her lest by her continual coming she weary me."

Jesus taught everything by telling parables. He only taught two parables on prayer, and both have the same lesson: never stop praying until the answer comes. It's not that God is like the neighbor or the unjust judge; He contrasts them. If these people got what they needed from such uncaring people, how much more will your Heavenly Father, who is full of compassion, give you what you ask for?

So pray the word of God until the answer comes. And ask others to join you. Agreement prayer is powerful. That's where the family of God comes in. Jesus said, "If two of you agree on earth concerning anything that they ask, it will be done for them by My Father in heaven" (Matt. 18:19). A three-fold cord is not easily broken. Prayer requests are good. Get others to pray with you.

This will get you started. Study and pray the word. And keep doing it. And get others to join you. Then you will be amazed at what God will do. It's a lifestyle, not a life preserver. Don't just pray in an emergency, pray without ceasing.

HOW TO LIVE THE CHRISTIAN LIFE

Give

Give and it will be given to you; good measure, pressed down, shaken together and running over...
—Luke 6:38

This little four-letter word sums up what *God* is all about, *love* is all about, *faith* is all about, and what *duty* is all about. This word is *the key to being saved, revival, health, and wealth.* It is relevant in every situation for every person. It will bring revival to your soul, friendship, and anything else you want. It's a word everybody understands, a sentence in itself. It is the *key to life* in the physical and spiritual realm. It is the word *G-I-V-E.*

Give is the key to God and knowing God. We are all sinners. We have taken from Him what belongs to Him—ourselves. This is called sin. All have sinned. And the payment for sin is death. We cannot do anything about this. It has already happened. But God did something about it. "For God so loved the world He gave..." God gave Jesus to die for our sins. There is no salvation apart from this. Christ gave His life that we might live forever. And then the resurrected Christ gives eternal life to all who give their lives to Him. God gives and we give—*that* is salvation. Give Him your heart and life, and He will give you abundant and eternal life.

I. G-I-V-E Is a *Personal* Word.

Jesus said, "Give, and it shall be given unto you…"

It includes every person. There is no subject to this verb in Luke 6:38. It includes everybody. Everyone is to give. Give what? There is no direct object. We are to give everything. More specifically, we are to give what we want, sow what we want to reap. "Give, and it shall be given unto you." What shall be given unto you? Whatever you give. "Whatever a man sows that shall he also reap" (Gal. 6:7). Stewardship includes *all* commodities. We are to give all we are and all we have. The word G-I-V-E is all *inclusive*.

This word from Jesus is *imperative*. It's a command. There are no options available. We either give or we disobey God. It is also *continuous*. A very literal translation: "You all must be always continually giving." Giving must become an attitude, a lifestyle, a way of thinking and living. It is also *unconditional*. There is no *if* before or after this command. There are no loopholes. Nobody can say, "But I have nothing to give." Thus, the command to give is to everyone, regarding everything, continuously, without condition.

II. G-I-V-E Is a *Practical* Word

Within that one little word is the key to the mysteries of the universe. All of nature operates under its law. The tree exists to produce (give). So does the Earth itself. And the sun: it gives light to us. We were made to give. The spirit realm operates under the same law. God gives, and we live as we give. Begin to hoard, and you begin to die: the cycle breaks down for you.

But wisdom does not dictate giving indiscriminately. Where do we begin? When and how much do we give? That is left up to us. The place to begin your giving is the place where you are experiencing your greatest need. Sow what you need to reap.

If you are experiencing an unmet need, you are having a giving problem. If you are not receiving, then something is wrong with your giving. Need time? Not enough time in your day? Well, you will never have more of it. The problem? You are not giving enough time away. Give God more time in your day. Tithe your time. Next, give some time daily to others. If Jesus's words are true, you will be given more time!

Need energy? Are you tired, drained, worn out all the time? The cure? Exercise. Lack of muscle comes from not using them. Use them. Give some energy and you be given energy. Need money? Tithe and give offerings. "Give and it shall be given unto you." Jesus Himself uttered these immortal words.

III. G-I-V-E Is a *Possible* Word

God always enables what He commands. Lazarus couldn't of his own ability come forth from the tomb. But when Jesus said to, he did. What Christ demands, He backs it by His dynamic. Therefore, we are without excuse. Give what you have.

IV. G-I-V-E Is a *Profitable* Word

Look at the promise attached to this command: "And it shall be given to you." He would not have made this promise if it were not so. He will keep His promise. Our concern is to do the command, trusting His resources. He will do His part. The promise to the giver is that he will receive abundantly. Yes, we are to expect to receive more than we give. That is faith. We expect God to keep His word.

Jesus uses four phrases to describe the profit we get:

1. Good measure
2. Pressed down
3. Shaken together
4. Running over

Let's look at *The law the harvest* in "Whatever a man sows that will he also reap" (Gal. 6:7).

Sowing is giving. Sowing the seed is to lose it, to bury it, to give it away.

There are three parts to this law of the harvest:

1) We always reap *what* we sow. "Whatever a man sows," it says. Sow corn, reap corn. Sow peas, reap peas. Sow love, reap love. Sow anger, reap anger. Sow $100 bills... This is an unbreakable law of the universe. If we sow good seed, we reap good seed. If we sow bad seed, then we reap bad seed. We will reap what we sow. Nobody ever sowed potatoes and harvested asparagus. You get out of something what you put in.

2) We reap *more* than we sow. "May He who supplies the seed, multiply the seed" (2 Cor. 9:10–11).

   This is what makes giving profitable. It is a law that cannot be broken. Plant a single grain of corn, and up comes a stalk with four ears of corn, each containing scores of grains of corn. If this were not the case, there would be no vegetable gardens or farming.

   It is equally true of other things. Sow a little, reap a lot. This is a law written within the very framework of the universe. It works for corn. It works for money. It works for everything. Nowhere in the Bible in there a command to give without a promise of abundant return on the investment.

3) We reap *later* than we sow. "In due season we will reap if we do not lose heart" (Gal. 6:9).

   There is a time process involved. Farmers don't plant one morning and harvest that afternoon. It takes months. It takes time to reap what you've sown. So give it time. This is where faith comes in. Can you trust God to bring in a harvest? Farmers have been doing it since the dawn of time. Christians must do it too. And as the farmer expects a harvest, so must we. We usually say to God, "If you give, I'll give." He says, "You have got it backwards." After you give, it will be given to you, press down, shaken together, and running over.

God wants us to abound in His provision. That's why He tells us to give. "My God shall supply all your needs according to his riches in glory by Christ Jesus" (Phil. 4:19).

Unfortunately, this is the hardest thing for us to believe. We find it easy to trust Him to take us to heaven when we die, but hard to believe He can take care of us here if we give.

V.   The Place Giving Is to Start

The Tithe. One does not really get into giving until after the tithe (10 percent of your gross income, after deducting what it cost you to make that money, i.e., business expenses, etc.) "Tithing is a debt I owe. Giving is a seed I sow."

> Will a man rob God?
> Yet you have robbed Me!
> But you say,
> "In what way have we robbed You?"
> In tithes and offerings.
> You are cursed with a curse,
> For you have robbed Me,
> Even this whole nation.
> Bring all the tithes into the storehouse,
> That there may be food in My house,
> And try Me now in this,"
> Says the Lord of hosts,
> "If I will not open for you the windows of heaven
> And pour out for you such blessing
> That there will not be room enough to receive it.
> "And I will rebuke the devourer for your sakes,
> So that he will not destroy the fruit of your ground,
> Nor shall the vine fail to bear fruit for you in the field,"
> Says the Lord of hosts;
> "And all nations will call you blessed,
> For you will be a delightful land,"
> Says the Lord of hosts.
> (Mal. 3:8–12)

We do harm to ourselves by giving *only* the tithe. The tithe is the beginning. If we don't tithe, we rob God. Many church members are living in stolen homes, driving stolen cars, wearing stolen clothes. They bought those things with the tithe they stole from God.

You cannot expect to have success with your money if you will not tithe. Some apparently are, but the final judgment is not in. Some who do not tithe have plenty, but they will pay at the judgment.

All the promises of provision in the Bible are conditional (Matt. 6:33, Luke 6:38, Phil. 4:19). Even the love of God in this sense is conditional: "So let each one give as he purposes in his heart, not grudgingly or of necessity; for God loves a cheerful giver" (2 Cor. 9:7). Our responsibility, by grace, is to meet the conditions. When we do, God will abundantly reward.

VI. Closing Comments

A. God owns all the wealth in the world. "The earth is the Lord's, and all its fullness, the world and those who dwell therein" (Ps. 24:1). Technically speaking, we do not just owe God our tithes, we owe Him everything because He has given and will give us all we have. "It is God who gives you the power to get wealth" (Deut. 8:18).

B. God wants His wealth in circulation.

> A bell is not a bell until you ring it,
> a song is not a song until you sing it,
> love in your heart wasn't put there to stay,
> love isn't love until you give it away.

The nature of true wealth is such that it can't be stored. The moment it is stored, it loses its value. The world says,

> Get all you can,
> Can all you get,
> Sit on the lid,
> And poison the rest.

Man has become a greedy getter instead of a gracious giver (like God). God will entrust to us as much as we can be trusted to put into circulation for His glory and the blessing of others.

C. God has put all of His wealth at man's disposal.

We are stewards of God's estate (1 Cor. 4). A steward is one who manages another's property. God will require an accounting of us, His stewards. "Let a man consider us as servants of Christ and stewards of the mysteries of God. It is required in stewards that one be found faithful" (1 Cor. 4:1–2).

D. The way to appropriate God's wealth is to *give*. Living things give and receive, and in this blessed cycle there is the perpetuation of life.

E. We are to give, not according to our actual wealth, but according to God's actual wealth.

There is such a thing as *Reason Giving*—give only what you can afford to give based on human calculation. This is not giving by faith, which is giving by revelation.

There is such a thing as *Revelation Giving*—giving what Gods says based on His power to provide, depending on His provision. This is giving by faith. Jesus praised the widow who gave two mites as giving more than anyone else gave that day. The widow gave Elisha all she had, not a rational thing to do.

F. Practical Pointers

Make a practice of giving away something you like. Preface it with a doxology of praise.

a) Entrust the totality of yourself and your possessions to the Lord.

b) List what you have, everything: body, strength, family, income, friends, achievements, things, pastimes, hobbies, plans, everything you possess. Say, "None of these are mine. They are all yours, Lord." He may come calling for any of these at any time. That's His prerogative, for it all belongs to Him.

c) Reckon upon God as your total resource, refusing every horizontal source as a final means of supply. When you become available in all you are to Him, He becomes available in all He is to you.

d) Begin to give from your new supply source, asking for a word about where to begin now. (You don't have to pray about tithing because that is a command from God.)

e) Expect God to work on His behalf in your circumstances in an obvious fashion. Expect divine intervention as you begin to give and He leads.

HOW TO LIVE THE CHRISTIAN LIFE

The Role of the Holy Spirit in Living the Christian Life

If by the Spirit you put to death the deeds of the body, you will live; for as many as are led by the Spirit of God, these are the sons of God.

—Romans 8:13–14

W e cannot live the Christian life without being led and empowered by the Holy Spirit. We cannot even be a Christian without the Holy Spirit giving us life in the new birth (John 3:5). "Now if anyone does not have the Spirit of Christ, he is not His" (Rom. 8:9).

We can't know God without knowing the Holy Spirit because the Holy Spirit is God (Acts 5:3–4). He is the third member of the Trinity. "The grace of the Lord Jesus Christ, and the love of God, and the communion of the Holy Spirit be with you all. Amen" (2 Cor. 13:14). He has all the attributes of God: He is eternal, omnipresent, omniscient, and omnipotent (Heb. 9:14, Ps. 139:7–13, 1 Cor. 2:10, Luke 1:35 respectively).

He brings us to Christ. He convicted us of our sins (John 16:8–10), lives in us (1 Cor. 6:19), and reveals everything we need to know about the Savior (John 16:13–14). We would know nothing of Jesus had the Spirit of God not made Him known to us. We can't see the life, death, resurrection, and ministries of Jesus to and for us in any way that would benefit us unless the Spirit shows these things to our hearts. He convinces us of our need for the Savior and then shows us the Savior. When we are born of the Spirit, we can see the kingdom of God.

The Holy Spirit wrote the Bible (2 Pet. 1:21). *Inspiration* is everything we need to know about God and what God requires of us is recorded infallibly for us by the Spirit of God in the Holy Bible. *Illumination* is the Spirit taking what He has written and making it known to the regenerate Christian. The Spirit also speaks directly to our spirits, but never contrary to anything He has written in the Word (Acts 13:2). He communes with us.

He is the key to living the Christian life: to commune and fellowship with the Spirit (2 Cor.13:14), be led by the Spirit (Rom. 8:14), baptized by Jesus with the power of the Spirit (Acts 1:8), be filled with the Spirit (Eph. 5:18), by the Spirit put to death the deeds of the flesh (Rom. 8:13), and to be consciously aware of His presence and voice in our spirits. To have God living inside of you and knowing it is the greatest blessing and the only way to live the Christian life. He is essential to walking with God.

Because He has no physical body like Jesus, He sometimes reveals Himself in symbolic ways. He is like Water (John 7:37–38), Fire (Isa. 4:4, Exod.13:21), Wind (John 3:8; Acts 2:2; Ezek. 37:9–10, 14), Oil (Ps. 45:7), Rain and Dew (Ps. 72:6, 68:9, 133:3), Dove, therefore gentle (Matt. 3:16), Voice (Isa. 6:8), and a Seal (Eph. 1:13–14). He is everything we need to live the Christian life. Everything.

He lives in the church. "Do you not know that you (plural) are the temple of God and that the Spirit of God dwells in you" (1 Cor. 3:16). He oversees the church (Acts 20:28), gives spiritual gifts (1 Cor. 12:4–11), teaches the members (John 14:26), calls people to the ministry (Acts 13:2–4), the source of our liberty (2 Cor. 3:17–18), unity (Eph. 4:3–4), and fellowship (Phil. 2:1). He edifies the church (Acts 9:31).

If you want to know God, then you have to get to know the Holy Spirit. He is in you, in your spirit, the deepest part of your being. Funny that someone can live in the same house as you and you still not know Him, but it's true. He can live in one room and you live your life in other rooms and never even speak to Him.

He is sensitive; He can be offended. He can be grieved by our carelessness toward Him and neglect of Him (Eph. 4:30). He can be *quenched* by our resisting His leading (1 Thess. 5:19). He can be lied to, resisted, insulted, undervalued, and blasphemed (Acts 5:3–4, 7:51, 8:19–20; Heb. 10:29; Heb. 6:4–6; and Matt.12:31 respectively). But He is the source of love: He puts the love of God in our hearts (Rom. 5:5). We would not know the love of God nor the grace of our Lord Jesus Christ if it were not for the communion with and the ministry of the Holy Spirit to our hearts (2 Cor.13:14).

He produces in us everything that God requires of us, the fruit of the Spirit (Gal. 5:22–25). His presence gives us love, joy, and peace. He gives us all the benefits of knowing God.

To live the Christian life we need to be constantly communing with the Holy Spirit. We need to get to know the Holy Spirit. How do you do that? The same way you get to know any other person: spend time with Him, talk to Him, listen to Him, rejoice with Him, trust Him. He is the only God you will know until Jesus comes back. Let your spirit commune with Him in tongues. "They were filled with the Holy Spirit and began to speak with tongues as the Spirit gave them utterance" (Acts2:4). "He who speaks in a tongue does not speak to men, but to God. I wish you all spoke with tongues. For if I pray in a tongue, my spirit prays" (1 Cor.14:2, 5, 14). Speak to Him and listen to His voice. We live by the Spirit as we commune with Him. Receive Him as you would a friend. He is the Spirit of Christ in you. His power will enable you to live the Christian life.

HOW TO LIVE THE
CHRISTIAN LIFE

Flesh versus Spirit
(Galatians 5:13–24)

Freedom is the most valuable and costly commodity on earth. People would rather die than live in slavery. Nobody ever expressed it more eloquently than Patrick Henry: "Give me liberty or give me death." War is not the worst thing there is; slavery is. William Wallace in the movie *Braveheart* died crying, "Freedom!" That has been the human heart cry for thousands of years. But only a sad few have ever lived free. America has always been the land of the free. We are not imperialists; we are liberators. And God has blessed America because of it.

The Christian life is one of liberty, but nothing is more difficult to have and hold as religious freedom. We are constantly swinging from bondage to the flesh to bondage to the law, and the puppeteer is none other than Satan himself: "The whole world lies under the sway of the wicked one" (1 John 5:19). Freedom of the spirit is more precious than physical freedom. Paul was in prison and wrote letters of joy and victory to churches.

Liberty is the theme of this letter to the Galatians, and in it he writes much on the themes of bondage and freedom, using stories from the Old Testament to illustrate the difference. The Galatians had become believers and had thus been set free. "Stand fast therefore in the liberty by which Christ has made us free, and do not be entangled again with the yoke of bondage" (5:1). They were battling against the two-fold cord of slavery that is not easily broken: licentiousness and legalism. On the left is bondage to the flesh. It poses as freedom, but it is a horrible bondage to the "flesh" that every Christian has because he is still living in an unredeemed body. To compensate for this license to sin, moralists proposed the law as the only antidote to this poison. So we have license to the flesh on the left and legalism by the law on the right. Liberty lies in the middle.

I.   Our Calling (v.13)

People sometimes tell me they don't know their calling in life. I tell them I can tell them. Please do, they say. Every Christian's calling is to liberty. That's exactly what it says: *"For you, brethren, have been called to liberty."* This is the call of God on our lives—to live free, because we were born free. The Spirit of God and the gospel have set us free from bondage to the flesh and the law (16, 18, 24). We are free because of our calling in Christ. Everybody lives by the law, the flesh, or the Spirit. Only the Spirit gives liberty (Rom. 8:5).

II.   Our Caution

The caution is to make sure we do not use this liberty as an opportunity to the flesh. As a free man we may sell ourselves into bondage and actually not live as free man. We can put ourselves in prison and lock the door behind us, much like Odom in Mayberry used to do on the *Andy Griffith Show*. One wife asked her husband what he was going to do on his day off, and he replied, "Fix Emily's bike and take Josh to the museum." She replied, "Doesn't sound like a very exciting way to spend your day off." He said, "It is if you love your kids." We must not use our liberty to hurt other people or do wrong but to love and serve them.

III.   Our Commandment (13–14)

"But through love serve one another. For all the law is fulfilled in one word, even in this: 'You shall love your neighbor as yourself.'" This is

the commandment that sets us free. Everything God requires of us is found in this one word. Everything.

I went to this one church and a telephone man came to hook me up with a new line. As he was working outside, I went to him and began to witness to him. He stopped me and said, "Listen, preacher, let's get something straight. I've been to all the churches in this town and asked the pastors to tell me what I need to do to be a good church member. They gave me a list of things, and each time I looked at it and thought, I can't do all this." I told this man that I had some good news for him. There was only one thing he had to do to be a good church member where I pastored—love. Just one thing, one word, one four-letter word—*love*! I guess by then it was too late, because I never saw him again. Our calling and commandment in life is to love others.

Galatians 5:15 pictures people not loving one another, like wild beasts fighting each other, and they fight with their mouths. So do we. Children tend to think very literally. Can you imagine what they must think when we talk about backbiting? Paul warns us that if we indulge in biting one another, we just might end up devouring and consuming one another. Cannibals! Eating our own kind. This is the activity of the flesh.

IV. The Conflict (16–17)

Here's the meat of the message, the point of the passage. There's a war going with every believer, a conflict of monumental proportion. It's the flesh versus the Spirit. The word *Spirit* could be a little spirit, meaning our own regenerated good spirit that the Holy Spirit makes alive to God at our new birth. I think it's a little *s* because the Holy Spirit would have no trouble defeating our flesh. It'd be like me fighting the heavyweight champion of the world. Only two hits and it's over. He hits me, and I hit the floor! Whether it's a little *s* or a big *S*, the results are the same. There's a war going on inside of every believer: flesh versus spirit. The flesh is opposed to the spirit. Opposition to doing what God wants is in all of us.

V. The Conquest (18)

Only the Holy Spirit can overcome this opposition. Our will power is never enough. In Romans 7:15–19, Paul states that he couldn't find it in himself to do what he wanted and he finds that what he doesn't want to do he does. We can't will ourselves out of the flesh. I can will to fly like Superman, but I can't do it. I want to be spiritual, but I can't. Not by myself. It takes the Holy Spirit filling and energizing my spirit. What we need is not freedom to sin without the guilt or consequences or another set of principles to live by. What we need is a Savior. Yes, Christians still need a Savior. It's not law or just another decision that can help. God, our deliverer, helps.

Note the order here and the all-inclusiveness of this passage concerning deliverance from our slaveries. The order is walk by the Spirit and then we will not fulfill the lusts (desires) of the flesh. We don't stop walking in the flesh and then we can walk in the Spirit. That's getting it backward. We must inhale before we can exhale. In verse 16 the Spirit delivers us from the flesh. In verse 18, He delivers us from the law. The Holy Spirit gives us freedom from both these horrible bondages. He does this through the word He speaks to our hearts.

Which bondage is worse, law or flesh, legalism or licentiousness? Legalism is worse than the flesh because the legalist, relying on the law, thinks he doesn't need grace or help. He is self-righteous, self-confident, and self-sufficient. When Jesus came, He was received by the fleshly crowd. Sinners heard Him gladly. But He was crucified by the legalist crowd. Paul experienced the same thing. The elder brother was last seen outside the father's house while the forgiven prodigal brother was inside partying with the rest of his family and friends.

VI. The Crucifixion (19–24)

We cannot defeat the flesh in us because the flesh *is* us and because the flesh has already been defeated—at the cross. When Christ died, *He died for our sins* and that freed us from the *penalty* of sin. But also, when He died *we died with Him* and that freed us from the *p*ower of sin. This is what is taught in this amazing paragraph. (Read Romans 6:1–7 for a detailed explanation of this.) This is Paul's theme and gospel for the believer. He had already mentioned it in Galatians 2:20 where he says, "For I have been crucified with Christ, nevertheless I live." There is no freedom without the gospel and the Holy Spirit. But first Paul makes clear what he means by the flesh and the Spirit. What are we freed from, and what are we free to do?

A. *The Flesh* (Gal. 5:19–21). There are sensual sins, supersti-tious sins, and social sins. The social sins are by far the most plentiful. He uses nine different words to say the same thing. *Just like the legalist, those who walk in the flesh cannot get along with others.* They hate, get angry, divide, create strife, envy, and are full of selfish ambitions. They always want their own way. It's their way or the highway, and you can hit the road.

Differences don't divide people. Not theological differ-ences or personal preferences. My wife and I are different. First, she's a woman and I'm a man! But our differences do not divide us. The flesh divides people, not differences. Paul closes this section by stating that those who live this way are not saved.

B. *The Spirit* (22–24). As we abide in Christ, the Holy Spirit produces godlike qualities in us and we become more like Jesus. (This fruit of the Spirit is a perfect picture of Christ.) Those in the Spirit love others, are at peace with others, and rejoice in the Lord and others. They are long-suffer-ing, kind, good, and faithful. This is how we are to live the Christian life. We are freed from the law and the flesh to walk in the Spirit.

VII. The Contrast

The contrast between the flesh and the Spirit is obvious. Anybody should be able to tell the difference with half their brain tied behind their back. But alas! How many cannot tell the difference? Someone comes to you gossiping and trash talking others with an obvious spirit of strife, and you just blindly follow them. It's easy to tell if someone is in the Spirit or in the flesh. The flesh is obvious. Judge the tree by its fruit. These people live in sin and divide churches, friends, and families. Don't listen to them, and don't join them. Rebuke them!

One of the most important statements in this passage is "Against such there is not law." If we have the fruit of the Spirit, we need no law. We are free because God Himself lives in us. It was a wonderful day when I realized the only thing God made me and called me to do is love. That's my job and purpose in life. That is all I am supposed to be doing. Through love, serve one another. Licentiousness, legalism, liberty! But wait, there's one more, and it's above them all. *Love!* The Spirit and the Gospel produces love. It's obvious.

HOW TO LIVE THE CHRISTIAN LIFE

Know, Reckon, Present

> Know *this, that our old man was crucified with Him, that the body of sin might be done away with, that we should no longer be slaves to sin.* Reckon *yourselves to be dead to sin but alive to God.* Present *yourselves to God as being alive from the dead, and your members as instruments of righteousness to God.*
> —Romans 5:19, 6:1–14

If you are a Christian, this is the most important message you will ever read, because it comes from the most important verses in the entire Bible for the believer, because we cannot possibly live the Christian life without having victory over the flesh which is the great enemy that will never leave us until we die. Kids in school will raise their hands and ask if the material I'm covering will be on the test. That's a loaded question. It means that if I say no, they are going to check out and ignore what I am about to teach. Well, the material I am about to cover will be on your test—daily—for the rest of your life. To live the Christian life, you need this more than anything else.

If we are to live the Christian life, we need to be delivered from what the Bible calls the *flesh*, which is in opposition to the Spirit, both the Holy Spirit and our own regenerated spirit (Gal. 5:17). It is the enemy of God and our greatest enemy (Satan is God's enemy), resisting everything God wants for us and wants to do in and through us. We cannot live the Christian life and live under the power of the desires of our flesh.

And we will not. God has insured that by the gospel. Two things happen when we are saved: (1) Christ comes to live in us, and (2) We are put into Christ. Christ is in us and we are *in Christ*. This second part is what Paul expounds in Romans 6–7. Indeed, it is his favorite phrase to explain our union with Christ in salvation.

In Romans 5 Paul begins to explain the doctrine of union, or identification, as some theologians call it. He says that we got lost by something someone else (Adam) did and we got saved by something some else (Christ) did (v. 19). Then in chapter 6 he anticipates an argument: "If I became lost because of what Adam did and saved by the grace of God because of what Christ did, then it must not make any difference what I do." And so he writes, "What shall we say then? Shall we continue in sin that grace may abound?" (6:1).

The word *sin* here is a noun. It is not a verb. He is not talking about something we do. He is not asking shall we continue to sin. He begins that subject in 6:15 where he asks, "What then? Shall we sin...?" That is a verb. In verse 1 he uses the noun form of the word *sin*. The noun sin means it is something. What is it? It is the sin nature that every human inherited in Adam. When Adam sinned, we all sinned because we were in him when he sinned. What happened to him happened to everyone in him. That's the doctrine of union that Paul leans heavily on in this passage and in his theology.

I have four daughters. What would have happened to them if I had died when I was eight years old? They would have died too. Why? Because they were in me when I died. That's their identification with me. In the same way, when Adam died to God, everybody in him died to God. And part of that death is the sin nature. We are not sinners because we sin; we sin because we are sinners. And we are sinners because we are in Adam, and what happened to him happened to everyone in him. Adam became a sinner by nature, and we are born sinners by nature. We are "by nature children of wrath" (Eph. 2:3). At the new birth in Christ, we get a new nature, one that is holy like God. Our spirits are regenerated in the likeness of the Christ.

Some people think that Christians have two natures in them: a good nature and a sin nature. That is not true, and Paul is going to say that it's not true in this important passage. Sin is the sin nature. So Paul asks, shall we continue to live according to the sin nature because of the grace of God? His answer is the strongest possible negative in the Greek language. Don't even think about it. Perish the thought. How dare you even think that thought! *Certainly not!* This can never be! And then he explains why he used such a violent negative.

To overcome sin, the sin nature, the flesh in our lives, Paul gives us three things to do. These things automatically happen when we are converted because we are in Christ. They are powerful, and these things are true even for baby believers. However, as we grow older and up in the Lord, God will no longer carry us about, feed, clothe, and clean us. As we mature, He, like any good father, wants us to take on these responsibilities for ourselves. Something is severely wrong with a teenager who can't feed himself or clean his own room! So God will back off and tell us how to do things. These three things we must do if we are to live the Christian life.

I.   *Know* (v. 3–10)

Everything begins with knowledge. If you don't know, you can't grow. I sometimes suffer from vertigo, have for years. But recently I know I didn't want to take any more meds for this, which basically knocked me out. I called a doctor friend of mine, and he told me about a maneuver that might help. I tried it, and *bam*! No more vertigo! I wish I had known this years ago. To be saved, we must come to the knowledge of the truth of the gospel (1 Tim. 2:4). To be delivered from the flesh, we must know some things.

Paul says in Romans 6:3, "Do you not know…?" In case they forgot, he tells them again. He had just said, "How shall we who died to sin live any longer in it?" And how did we die to sin? Verse 3 explains it. What he explains we need to know. We desperately need to know. We cannot live the Christian life without knowing some things.

Although he does not mention it in chapter 6, he has prior to this informed us of something extremely important that we need to know. It is the truth about justification. In Romans 4:5–8 he tells us that God justifies the ungodly totally apart from works by virtue of their faith in Christ. Before being declared right with God (the meaning of justification), we could do nothing but sin. We were in sin, so we could do nothing but sin. Being under the power of our sin nature, "There is none righteous, none who seeks after God, none who does good, no, not one" (Rom. 3:9–12). "All our righteousness's are like filthy rags" (Isa. 64:5).

As a lost sinner in Adam, we can't do anything right. A sobering truth for sure. That's why we must be born again and we must be put into Christ. The other side of that coin is, the believer, the saint, can't do anything wrong. Not as far as God is concerned. He is totally justified. "There is no condemnation to those who are in Christ Jesus" (Rom. 8:1). As far as God is concerned, we are righteous because the righteousness of Christ has been imputed to us. The Bible never calls a saint a sinner. As far as fellowship and discipline is concerned, we can commit acts of sin. That's why we have 1 John1:9. But as far as justification is concerned, we never sin. As far as God is concerned, the sinner in Adam can do nothing right and the saint in Christ can do nothing wrong. As far as sanctification (the theme of Romans 6–8) is concerned, we cannot live in *sin*. The sin nature has died with Christ. We need to know this.

What God is going to do in sanctification is make us to be what He has declared us to be. "So also, by one Man's obedience (Jesus in the gospel) many will be made righteous" (Rom. 5:19). Justification means to be declared *righteous;* sanctification means to be *made* righteous. What God declares by virtue of the death and resurrection of Christ, He makes so through that same death and resurrection.

What the Scripture is getting at here in Romans 6, the thing He wants us to know, is that when we became Christians, the Spirit of God baptized us into Christ. "Do you not know…" (6:3). Don't let the word *baptize* throw you. There is no water here. The Spirit immerses the believer into Christ (1 Cor. 12:13). He is no longer considered by God to be in Adam. He is in Christ and a new creation (2 Cor. 5, 17).

Here's the point. What happened to Christ happened to everyone in Him. What happened to Him? He died. "Therefore, we were buried with Him through baptism into death." When He died, we died. Why? Because we were in Him. If I put a $100 bill into my Bible, wrap it with duct tape, and then send that Bible to China, what happens to the money? It goes to China. Why? Because it is in the Bible. If God put us into Christ and He died, what happened to us? We died. But we didn't stay dead because He didn't stay dead. "For if we have been united together in the likeness of His death, certainly we also shall be in the likeness of His resurrection." This is what prevents us from continuing in sin. Impossible! Perish the thought!

In verse 6 Paul puts it like this: "Knowing this, that our old man was crucified with Him, that the body of sin might be done away with, that we should no longer be slaves to sin." The *old man* here is our sin nature. It is what we have because we are were born of Adam. When the *last Adam* died, we died with Him. When the *second Man* rose, we rose with Him (1 Cor. 15:45–47). In Christ we are a new creation. Our old man was crucified with Him. What is the effect of our sin nature dying with Christ? Our body of sin became unemployed.

The *body of sin* refers to our present natural body, which, while not inherently sinful, is still unredeemed and living in this corrupt world. The body is like a TV, or a computer, or a gun. It can be used for good or bad. It is neutral of a sort. But it still has a brain and members that are programmed for unbelief and sin in which we lived before we got saved and still has those propensities even after we are born again.

"Done away with" does not mean annihilated or destroyed. This same word is used of Satan, and he certainly has not been eliminated. It means to be unemployed or sidelined. Our body of sin is now unemployed as far as sin is concerned. We no longer owe sin our service. We are no longer its slave.

Christians do not have two conflicting natures battling for control of our lives. We have one new holy nature, but it is incarcerated in unredeemed flesh. Even though the human body is not inherently sinful (it can be presented to God for His service, Rom. 12:1) it is still unredeemed (Rom. 8:23) and thus has all the inclinations of the sinful self we lived in before we were saved. Sanctification (power over the flesh) is a sure thing, as saved people can attest to because of the change that has taken place in their lives.

But there comes a time in our growth as Christians when we must leave off being carried around by our Father and we must learn to walk on our own. To do that, to live the Christian life, we need to learn how this change has taken place and begin to take on our responsibility for living the Christian life. That's what Romans 6–8 is all about. God uses three words to explain our responsibility to live this life. The first is *know*.

We are dead to sin. He who has died with Christ is dead to sin and free from it. "He who has died has been freed from sin" (v. 7). I can fix it to where I will never sin again. How, you say. Be a good thing to know, wouldn't it? Here's how: put a gun to my head and blow my brains out. I would never sin again. Why? Cause I'd be dead. Dead people don't sin. In Christ we died to sin so we cannot live in sin. *Certainly not!* Know this, God put you into Christ. You are dead to sin and alive to God through the death and resurrection of Christ because you were in Him when He died and rose again. That's the truth. Reckon it to be so.

II. *Reckon*

This means to consider. The verb tense means to continually consider. Never let it out of your mind. The things that are true are to be reckoned true because they are true. We don't make something true by reckoning it to be true. We reckon it to be true because it is true. It is true that we are "dead indeed to sin, but alive to God in Christ Jesus our Lord." You can put that in the bank. Program it into your hard drive. Put it on your desktop. Victory over the flesh comes from continually reckoning yourself to be dead to sin and alive unto God through Christ.

Suppose I was to put a million dollars into your bank account. Would that bless you? Of course! Suppose you didn't know about it? Would it still bless you? No! You must know about something before it can be a blessing to you. Now suppose you had it in your bank account and knew it was there but never drew on that money? You never used your debit card or check book to actually buy anything? Would it do you any good? Of course not! Using it is the reckoning of it. Your using it didn't put it into the bank. You use it because it is in the bank. Reckon is actually an accounting term used in the same way I've been describing what we do with the truth of the knowledge we've been reading about. When the banker writes it in the books or puts it in the computer, it's there. Whether you know about it or not, it is there. That's the truth. You have died with Christ to sin. That's the truth. When you begin to use that debit card, you are reckoning the money is there and using it. When you reckon you are dead to sin and alive to God, you are using what Christ has given you. "Likewise, you also, reckon yourselves to be dead indeed to sin but alive to God in Christ."

III. *Present* (v. 13–14)

Since our body is unemployed as regards to sin (v. 6), what are we to do with it? Go to God's employment office and "present your-selves to God, as being alive from the dead, and your members as instruments of righteousness to God." We literally present our bodies to God. "Lord, here are my eyes. They are Yours. Use them as You will. I don't want to look at anything You don't want me to look at, and I want to see what You want me to. Lord, here are my hands. Here is my mouth. Here is my brain, my feet, my everything. I pres-ent them to You as Your slave to do with as only You will." This is when the Spirit of Christ that is in us takes over with His power to enable us to live the Christian life.

There is one more thing not found in this passage, but it is located after another lengthy passage on the flesh. Coming out of

Romans 7 where Paul describes *sin* as keeping us from obeying God (7:18–19), his answer to the flesh is in Romans 8. There God adds the Holy Spirit to the gospel of Christ's death, burial, and resurrection as the answer to the flesh. In Romans 8:1–5, he describes those who are in Christ as those *"who do not walk according to the flesh, but according to the Spirit."* And he adds, "For the law of the Spirit of life in Christ Jesus has made me free from the law of sin and death." The answer to the flesh is the gospel and the Holy Spirit. We are in Christ, and He is in us. We must know these things, continually be reckoning them to be so, and then present our bodies to God for doing the will of God.

When I was in college, I was taking a nap on my bed one afternoon and Don knocked on my door, with a basketball under his arm. "Wanna shoot some hoops?" I looked at him and said sure. Don was a whale of a guy, slightly taller than I was but severely overweight. I thought I could run circles around this guy. I was pretty agile and fleet of foot, and so I accepted the challenge to get on the court with him. Well, I did. I took the ball out and ran like a racehorse around a statue. But I never was that good of a shooter. Not so with Don. He never missed. He slaughtered me, annihilated me, sent me to the house. I was embarrassed and vowed never to play basketball with him again.

The next day, while again resting on my bed, I thought, *What if by some miracle I could get Meadowlark Lemon inside of me so nobody could see this six-foot-six Harlem Globetrotter. And what if he could take over my body and do what he did so well. He was perhaps the greatest basketball player of all time. You'd have to see him to believe him. With all his entertaining antics on the floor he was still a great bb player. And then Don would come with his stupid ball that was as round as he was, tucked under his chubby arm.*

So I imagined it. We'd get on the floor, and he'd run up the score on me until finally I would take the ball out and say to Meadowlark who is inside of me, "Are you ready to take over, to take charge of my body?" And he would say yes. Then I would start drop kicking balls into the basket from half court, shooting them off my hip from the free throw line, and all the things that only the great

Globetrotter could do. Don would stand there, scratching his head and say, "You look like Terry Simpson, but you don't play basketball like Terry Simpson." And he would be right. I played basketball like Meadowlark Lemon. Why? Because he was in me, taking charge of my body.

That's exactly what the Spirit does. Miraculously, He is in me and nobody can see Him, but when I present the members of my body to Him, He takes over and helps me do things I could never do on my own. He helps me live the Christian life.

That's how the life is lived: *know*ing I am in Christ so that when He died to sin I died to sin, and when He rose, I rose to newness of life; and *reckon*ing this to be so; and finally *present*ing my body to Him for Him to live the Christian life through me.

We actually have to do these things, as often as needed, which would certainly include at least once a day. And since accountability is the key to everything, I want to suggest that you find someone you can make yourself accountable to and ask him or her to ask you often if you are doing these things on a daily basis. We need accountability.

Everybody is a slave. You're sitting next to one right now, if you're sitting next to anyone. You shaved one this morning, if you shaved this morning. Everyone is a slave. Romans 6:22 says, "But now having been set free from sin, and having become slaves of God..." God has rescued us from one slavery only to make us His slaves. Oh, benevolent change of masters. Emancipation from Master Sin, only to be made slaves of the wonderful Savior. Blessed slavery that is! Bondage to Jesus is sweet liberty indeed. It frees us *from* doing wrong *to* doing right.

Spurgeon put it like this:

> Man is born to be a servant, and a servant he must be. Who shall be his master? When we come from under the absolute power of sin we come at once into a like subjection to righteousness. As sin took possession of us and controlled our acts, so grace claims us as its own, takes possession of us, and rules us with an absolute sway.

Man passes from one master to another, but he is always in subjection. Free will I have often heard of, but I have never seen it. I have met the will, and plenty of it, but it has either been led captive by sin or held in the blessed bonds of grace. The passions drive it hither and thither like a rolling thing before a whirlwind; or the understanding sways it, and then, according as the understanding is darkened or enlightened, the will acts for good or evil. In any case, the bit is in its mouth, and it is guided by a power beyond itself.

Well put. Man was made to serve. But who shall be his master? There are only two possibilities: sin or God.

I used to meet with a bunch of fellas at a restaurant every morning to discuss "everything controversial." We talked religion and politics. They were atheists, agnostics, liberals, conservatives, Christians, and some who didn't know what they were. One of my favorite "antagonists" around the several tables was an atheist. We grew to respect and even admire each other for at least being keenly astute concerning the topics of discussion. One day I walked into the restaurant during the afternoon and he was sitting there with his daughter who was home from college. I walked up to them and (without introduction) asked, "What is the worst thing in the world?" He told his daughter who I was and then said, "War!" He proceeded to expound the evils of war. His daughter said she wasn't sure.

I told them it wasn't war, it was slavery, and that our Founding Fathers for instance had said things like, "Give me liberty or give me death." Furthermore, honorable men down through the ages had gladly gone to war to tear off the shackles of servitude to other men. Slavery was therefore worse than war. His daughter joined my side in the fray! He laughed and got up out of his seat at the table and hugged me. I'm not aware that we ever agreed on anything, but he appreciated my arguments and knew that I believed strongly what I believed. And he loved me for it. Well, I do agree with the honorable of this world. Slavery is worse than war. Patrick Henry had it right. Slavery is worse than death (by war).

I like to ask people, "Who is your worst enemy?" I get some good answers. The most popular one is "Satan." But Satan is God's enemy. We just got in the middle of the battle going on between them. Don't even think about saying your worst enemy is your spouse, or (if you are a teenager) your parents, or the IRS, or Muslim terrorists. The Bible teaches that *sin is our worst enemy*. Why? What will sin do to you? It will eventually kill you and send you to hell. Jesus said, "If your right eye causes you to sin, gouge it out and cast it from you, for it is better to enter into life maimed than to enter into hell whole." That makes sin a pretty serious enemy, wouldn't you say? It'll make you miserable before it brings you to the doors of death and hell. It divides homes, churches, nations, and the world. Sin is our worst enemy, but not because of any of those things. They are a by-product of the horrible thing that sin actually does.

Sin will take your freedom. It'll make you its slave. It will enslave you in the worst way. Let's look at some Scriptures: "That we should no longer be slaves of sin; For he who has died has been freed from sin; Therefore do not let sin reign in your mortal body, that you should obey it in its lusts; For sin shall not have dominion over you; you were slaves of sin; For when you were slaves of sin; But now having been set free from sin" (Rom. 6:6–7, 12, 17, 20, 22). And that's just a few, but they are all in the text we have come to in our studies.

Sin will take your freedom. Paul explains this in 7:19–20: "For the good that I will to do, I do not do; but the evil I will not to do, that I practice. Now if I do what I will not to do, it is no longer I who do it, but sin that dwells in me." *Sin will not let you do what you want to do. And it will make you do what you don't want to do.* Beloved, *that is slavery!* That is horrible bondage. Sin makes me do wrong and keeps me from doing right. As a believer I want to do right and I don't want to do wrong, but sin will not let me do right and always makes me do wrong.

Let me clarify. Exactly what is this evil enemy that lives within us? What is the sin that we are *certainly not* to continue in? What is sin? Sin is sometimes called the "sin nature" by Bible teachers, but the Bible's first name for sin is "sin." Sin is that about us which is wrong from birth and to the core. We are sin-ners. We are *in* sin and *under* sin (Rom. 3:9). Sin lives in us, in our mortal bodies. It makes us sinners, and it makes us sin.

The second most used term in the Bible for sin is "the flesh." It is called this because of its close, intimate association with our body. In fact, sin in us will not leave or die until our body dies. That's why the body eventually dies! And that's why the body is called "the body of sin" (6:6) and "the body of death" (7:24). And it is why sin is called "the flesh." Until the redemption of the body, sin will remain in our body.

The good news, however, is that we can get victory over it. It can be dethroned. Its power can be broken. This whole section of Romans (6–8) dealing with sanctification has to do with the dethroning of sin. Remember 5:21? "So that as sin reigned in death." Sin can only be dethroned by the reign of grace. "Even so grace might reign." Sin (the flesh) is conquered, not by eliminating sin (the sin nature) or by disciplining the body. We must *die* to it. *We* must die, and if we are to continue to live, we must be resurrected. We will literally and physically die one day, but this actually happens in the spirit *now*. That's what Romans 6–8 is all about. Physically speaking, when our body dies and we are raised with a glorified one, sin will be forever removed. But in our heart (spirit) we can be delivered through the death and resurrection of Christ. Right now. In this life.

In Romans 6, we are delivered from slavery to sin by the death of Christ, and in Romans 7 we are delivered from bondage to the law through the same death of Christ, the same gospel. In both cases, *we die*. We die because we are in Christ. Suppose your grandfather had died when he was but ten years old. Where would you be? Dead, of course. Why? Because you were *in* him when he was ten and died. Just like you were in Adam when he died. And in Christ when He died! We were baptized into Christ by the Holy Spirit, placed into Him so that when He died all those who were in Him died. And when He was resurrected, all who were in Him were resurrected. We are slaves to sin in our bodies and the only way out is to die. The good news is someone has already died in our place as us! We are dead. We are dead to sin. Already!

"Well," you might say, "if I'm so dead to sin, why do I have such a problem with it?" *Because you forget* (or haven't known), and you don't think about it enough. And you don't continually *present* your body to God as an instrument of righteousness. Here's exactly where the inspired pen of Paul helps. He explains how we can knowingly, continually and increasingly live in the victory of Christ's death and resurrection. We're coming to Romans 8:6 eventually, but I want to bring it up at this point in my discussion because it fits perfectly here. It says, "For to be carnally minded is death, but to be spiritually minded is life and peace." Wouldn't it be just like God to hang our deliverance from our greatest enemy on our continually being mindful of His greatest accomplishment, which was His victory over sin in the death and resurrection of His Son? Victory over our greatest enemy comes by being continually mindful of the greatest thing God has ever done. Think on these things (Christ's death and resurrection), and you will have life and peace. We are to live off the gospel. Only then will we have the peace of God in our lives as we live the crucified, resurrected, and Spirit-filled life.

The way to victory. Paul uses three verbs in Romans 6:4–13 to explain our part in the sanctifying process. God elects us without our cooperation, He redeems us and regenerates us without our even knowing it, and He will eventually resurrect us without our effort. But He does not sanctify us (at least not progressively) without our participation in the process. Our part, according to our text, is to *know, reckon,* and *present*. First comes faith (knowing), then comes believing (reckoning), and then repentance (presenting). These three words express everything we need to do. They are the whole counsel of God.

[The Bible will oftentimes use different words (synonyms) to say the same things. This shows the different facets and the richness and fullness of the things of the Spirit. Words are the best we have, but they are still poor transporters of the depth of the meanings of the things of God. We have to use many and varied ones to fully communicate the wealth of spiritual meanings. That's why the Bible is such a big book!]

Let's take a quick walk through this passage in Romans, pausing at each verb along the way. Beginning with 6:4, I want to point out that Paul lets us know we have a whole gospel. In Christ we have for ourselves not only a death to sin but also a resurrection to "newness of life." Our death is life-altering: it dethrones sin and enthrones grace. It makes us dead to sin, but it also makes us alive unto God. Baptized into Christ, *we* are dead and resurrected. Hallelujah! This resurrection is certain because we are in Christ who was crucified and raised. Verse 5 speaks of the resurrection of our bodies in the future for sure, but it also speaks of the resurrection of our spirits now. That's the point of the passage. "Shall we continue in sin?" has to do with *before* the bodily resurrection, not afterward.

Knowing (6:6). To walk with God we must know some things. No way around it. We must come to the knowledge of the truth—the truth of the gospel. Verse 6 has three closely related clauses. We are told that something happened, in order that something else might happen, in order that a third thing might happen. "Our old man was crucified with Him." The old man is what we were in Adam. *That old man was put to death. The old man is me. Sin is the old man's master.* In Christ, God no longer looks at us as being in Adam. We are in Christ. The "first man" was crucified, and the "second Man" was resurrected (1 Cor. 15:45–47). We need to know that. Everything depends on that truth and our knowledge of it. Grace cannot consistently reign in our lives, and sin cannot be dethroned and defeated without this knowledge.

"Our old man was crucified that the body of sin might be done away with…" "The body of sin" is our body. Because sin dwells in our mortal bodies, the body is called the body of sin. "*Done away with*" doesn't mean destroyed. It obviously hasn't been destroyed. This is the same word used in Hebrews 2:14, where it speaks of the death of Christ destroying the devil. He also has obviously not been destroyed. The old man was crucified with Christ, rendering our bodies inoperative to sin. Unemployed is a good translation.

Because our old man was crucified, our body is unemployed as far as sin is concerned. "That we should no longer be slaves of sin." Old Master Sin has no more legal claim on our bodies. We are dead to sin; therefore, our bodies are no longer legally, necessarily subservient to it. "For he who has died has been freed from sin."

Verses 8–10 simply reminds us of the inevitable consequence of dying with Christ: we were raised with Him. This is not a resuscitation. It is a bona fide resurrection, *never* to die again. If Christ dies no more, then those in Christ die no more. This is security! If *He died to sin once for all* and *He lives to God* forever, then so do those in Him. Know this! Learn it good. Get it down. Death no longer has dominion over Him or you. Therefore, sin no longer has dominion over you.

Reckoning (6:11). This is the second verb of responsibility. It means to consider. The verb tense means to continually consider. Never let it out of your mind. The things that are true are to be reckoned true because they are true. We don't make something true by reckoning it to be true. We reckon it to be true because it is true. It is true that we are "dead indeed to sin, but alive to God in Christ Jesus our Lord." You can put that in the bank. Program it into your hard drive. Put it on your desktop. Victory comes from continually reckoning ourselves to be dead to sin and alive unto God through Christ.

Presenting (6:13). If our body is unemployed as regards to sin, what are we to do with it? Go to God's employment office and "present yourselves to God, as being alive from the dead, and your members as instruments of righteousness to God."

Here's Romans 6 in a nutshell: *We cannot continue in sin because we died to sin. We cannot continue to sin because we obeyed from the heart (presented ourselves to God) and thus have been set free from sin and become slaves of righteousness.*

HOW TO LIVE THE
CHRISTIAN LIFE

Trust the Providence of God

*And we know that all things work together
for good to those who love God.*

—Romans 8:28

I.   We have the *providence* of God making all things work for our
good.

Right in the middle of this truthful passage on suffering (8:14–39) is
one of the most wonderful verses in the entire Bible: Romans 8:28. If
you believed this, nothing would get you down or make you quit. You
could endure anything if you knew that all things work together for
your good. Providence is God caring for and supervising His creation,
His mysterious behind-the-scenes sovereignty, overseeing everything
to insure the completion of His foreordained purposes. All of nature is
His chess pieces moved by the mysterious hand of Providence.

If we are going to live the Christian life, we must learn to trust
the providence of God in our sufferings and disappointments in life.
If we do not, we stand a chance of becoming mad at God or so dis-
illusioned with Him that we lose that closeness and intimacy with
Him that we need to effectively live the Christian life. We must come
to grips with God in the midst of our sufferings. This verse does
more than anything in the Bible to help us.

One of the biggest lies ever perpetrated is that all the Founding Fathers of the US were deists, the belief that God wound up the universe like a clock and does not interfere with mankind. He's just watching what they do. At the Constitutional Convention in 1787, there was almost total disagreement about how our nation should be set up. They were getting nowhere. Ben Franklin stood up and made this speech: "I have lived, sir, a long time, and the longer I live, the more convincing proofs I see of this truth—that god governs in the affairs of men. And if a sparrow cannot fall to the ground without his notice, is it probable that an empire can rise without his aid?" He proposed that they begin each day's deliberations with prayer for the hand of Providence to guide them. And they did.

It does not say that all things *are* good. All things are not good. Death is not; it's an enemy. Sin is not good. Disease is not good. Bad things are not good. It also does not say that God works all things for the good of all people. Not everything in everybody's life is going to work for their good. Good things can work for people's hurt. It's good to have a Bible, but if you ignore it, you'll wish you had never seen one. Some will suffer many things on this earth and then go to hell. All things are not good, and all things will not work together for good for everyone, only for those who love God and are fitting into His purpose.

II. How do we *know* all things work together for good?

   A. We know something of it from personal experience. Have you ever had a bad thing happen and you said, "I don't see how anything good could ever come out of this," only to look back later and see that good did come of it? A town in Alabama has a monument erected on the courthouse square of a boll weevil. After a few successive years of cotton crop failures due to the destructive eating habits of the boll weevil, the economy was in the tank and the county was in economic disaster. Finally, someone had the idea to begin raising peanuts. Their economy soared beyond anything imaginable when cotton was king. So they put up the memorial, not to the peanut but to the boll weevil! If it were not for the evil weevil, they would have never come to know the peanut and the economic boom that happened to their county.

B. All those times of troubles that resulted in terrific testimonies of victory in the Bible are tokens of what we'll see when we all get to heaven, where we'll understand it better. At that time we will see clearly that for those who loved God everything did indeed work for their good. Let's trust Him for that now.

We know it from the examples given to us in the Bible. The Bible not only says it is so, it shows it in almost every character in it. Take the worst things that happened in the OT and NT, and you see illustrations of this glorious truth. *Joseph* is the God-ordained promised leader of his famous family, yet he is sold by his own wicked brothers into slavery. Is this good? No! Can God cause this to work together for good for Joseph and the family? Yes, and He did. *Jesus* suffered as no one else ever has. Was it worth it? Did it work out for good? "Therefore, God has highly exalted Him…" (Phil. 2:5–11). God can take the evil of others and work it for good, which means, nothing the devil throws at you cannot be used by God for your good. Acts 2:23 and 4:27–28 shows clearly the hand of God in the crucifixion of Jesus by wicked men.

III. What makes all things work together for good? *God* does.

Some modern translations have Paul writing it this way: "God causes all things…" Those words are certainly in the heart and mind of the writer. They catch the meaning of the text. All things don't just work together for good on their own accord in and of themselves. The Bible teaches from cover to cover that God governs in the affairs of men. He sees to it that all things work together for good. The absence of "God" in this verse speaks of the providence of God. He hides Himself and works mysteriously through natural means. Only those who have eyes to see can detect that He is behind the scenes working His mysterious ways.

The book of Esther is the great example of the providence of God. Nowhere is God mentioned in that book and yet His providential hand is everywhere. God was in all the things that happened there, and He is in all the sufferings of our lives, making them all work together for our good.

No matter what comes into the life of a God-lover or is taken out, God causes it to work for good. Never forget that. What a truth to help you through the hard times. The good in everyone's life comes from God. Theology can be summed up simply with these words: God—good, devil—bad.

Have you ever seen those guys who can let you make any mark on their canvas and they can draw something beautiful and interesting out of it, incorporating the mark into their masterpiece? God can do that with a life that loves Him. You've had a divorce? Divorce isn't good. But God can work it for the good. You've had a death in the family? An accident? A financial setback? Whatever it is, God can cause good to come out of it. In fact, if you ever get down in the mouth, think of Jonah! He came out all right.

IV. What is *included* in the "all things"?

In the Greek *all things* mean "all things." Paul uses the word *panta*, which means wholly, entirely everything, by all means. It is emphatic in its meaning. All things are all things.

A. You can't name anything that is not included in all things. You can't name anything that God can't work for your good. You can't name anything that has, is, or will ever happen to you that God can't work for the good. Paul lists some things in this chapter: tribulation, distress, persecution, famine, nakedness, peril, sword, nor any other created thing (v. 35, 38–39).

B. Even sin? Your own sin? "Who loves God the most?" Jesus asked. The one who is forgiven the most. God can graciously cause even sin to work for good, but you might not like how He does it. Ask Jonah. He messed up, but Nineveh got saved. Ask Joseph. His brothers sinned, but he ended up on the throne.

C.   Even the sin of others against you! "So now it was not you who sent me here, but God." So said Joseph to those who had sinned against him by selling him into slavery. We are not at the mercy of the wicked hands of others. We who are God-lovers are at the mercy of the all-merciful God who overrules the wicked deeds of others against us. They do not have the last say, God does. The good God does.

D.   Write down anything, anything bad, in the margin of this sheet. I mean really bad. Rape. Humiliation. Theft. Maiming. Now, what you wrote down is included in the "all things." Go ahead, write something else down. Write as many bad things as you can imagine. They are all included in the all things.

V.   What *is* the good toward which all things work?

What's good for you might not be good for me and vice versa. I even know people who don't like fried chicken or chocolate! I think those things are very good. So what's the good toward which everything is working in the lives of everyone who loves God?

Well, it's *not* a life of comfort and ease, health and wealth, pleasure and power, fun and fame. The immediate context (v. 29–30) and the broader context will not permit that interpretation. Paul and the believers of his day certainly had none of those things. The last part of this chapter is taken up with the second type of suffering: persecution. Not only is the Christian not exempt from "the sufferings of this present time" that all people experience simply because they are part of the old creation, he is certainly not exempt from suffering because he is a Christian. He writes about being *killed all day long, tribulation, distress, persecution, famine, nakedness, peril and sword* (8:35–36). In another place, Paul wrote, "If any man will live godly in Christ Jesus, he will suffer persecution" (2 Tim. 3:12). Jesus said to rejoice when (not if) you suffer for righteousness sake. All believers suffer in some measure because they are living in a world of unbelief. Check out Romans 8:37 where Paul brings the Old (Ps. 44:22) and New Testament together under this theme: "For Your sake we are killed all day long; we are counted as sheep for the slaughter."

It's not that God doesn't bless us during the sufferings of this present time. We should thank God for all His blessings of peace and prosperity, health and happiness. These are good, and they are from God. But they are not what this passage is talking about. God obviously hasn't decreed every believer to a life of health and wealth, ease and comfort. He certainly hadn't the ones discussed in the last part of Romans 8. But He has predestined *"as many as He foreknew"* to something. What is it?

Our response to the pain in our lives is crucial. If we do not respond by thinking, speaking, and acting like Jesus, we may remain in the suffering until we do since that is the God-ordained purpose for it.

The good toward which all things are working together is not necessarily a life without loss. Then pray, tell what is it? The immediate context of verse 28 tells us. Verse 29 says, "For whom He foreknew, He also predestined to be conformed to the image of His Son..." The good toward which all things are working is our being conformed to the image of Christ, our being made more like Jesus. *That* is good, and it is good for everybody. No matter what happens, God is going to use it to make the believer more like Jesus in character, attitude, and action. And that is enough for everyone who loves God. Whatever needs to happen to me to make me more like Jesus Christ, let it happen. Whatever *has* happened to me, I receive it as a part of what God is using to make me like His Son.

Beloved, this is what salvation is all about: God making us more like Jesus. And He wastes nothing in the process. God will cause all things to work together for the good of those who love Him. When God doesn't make sense, think about the fact that He is not so much interested in your comfort and ease as He is your being made into His image: "That He might be the first born among many brethren."

VI. *For whom* does God cause all things to work for good?

Wouldn't you like this to be true of you and thus know that everything that has or ever will happen will be for your good? Would you like to be among those for whom God is working all things for good? Of course, you would! Nothing could be better. God takes anything and everything that happens to these people and turns it around for their good. Sign me up! Well, as I said, He doesn't do this for everyone; therefore, you want to be sure that you are one of the ones for whom this promise is true. Here are the people:

A. *God works all things for good to* those who love God.

Do you love God? Now don't ask yourself or your mother. Ask Him! Ask the One who says He does this wonderful thing. Then look up *His* answer. Jesus said these words in John 14:21: "He who has My commandments and keeps them, it is he who loves Me." "For this is the love of God, that we keep His commandments. This is love, that we walk according to His commandments" (1 John 5:3, 2 John 6). There you have it. Don't fool yourself into thinking that because you have this somewhat vague, sentimental, warm, fuzzy feeling for God that you truly love Him. Those who love Him are the ones who know and keep His commandments. Many people don't know or even care to know what His commandments are. They do not search the Scriptures to find out what pleases God. And they think they love God! You don't need to be wrong about whether you really love God or not. A lot depends on this. Everything depends on it.

B. *God works all things for good to* those who are the called according to His purpose.

He does this for the called. "To those who are called, Christ is the power of God and the wisdom of God" (1 Cor. 1:24). Is Christ your power and wisdom? Are you fitting into His purpose? Do you live for yourself or for God? You know He doesn't really care about your agenda, your time-oriented, vain purposes. It's "called according to His purpose." Do you live for His purpose or yours? Are you following the leadership of the Holy Spirit and thus proving yourself to be a bona fide child of God? (Rom. 8:14).

Now, wouldn't you like these things to be true of you? You'd be crazy not to want this. This is the only way to be a winner in the end. But you must make the necessary adjustments now. In the sandwich of life, there is a lot of bologna. Do you ever feel like your life should be listed in the Yellow Pages under "Junk"? The only place you don't feel like a loser is on the bathroom scales. You feel like a crumb at the bottom of the great cookie jar of life? Well, your responsibility is to love God with all your heart. And there is nothing unreasonable about this. It's the thing that makes more sense than anything else. We *should* love God. After all, He loves us. Enough to send His Son to die for our sins. We ought to love Him because He first loved us. How do we know that He loves us? "God demonstrated His own love for us, in that while we were yet sinners, Christ died for us" (Rom. 5:8).

HOW TO LIVE THE CHRISTIAN LIFE

Believe That God Is for You

If God is for us, who can be against us? He
who did not spare His own Son?
—(Romans 8:31–32)

If we are going to live the Christian, we must come to terms with pain, *"the sufferings of this present time"* (Rom. 8:18). In a perfect world, there would be no pain, no suffering. There would be no physical pain, emotional pain, death, disease, divorce, accidents, broken bones, or broken hearts. But as we all know, we do not live in a perfect world. Not yet! We live in a sinful world that has brought unbelievable pain and suffering upon itself. The whole of Romans 8:18–39 helps us learn how to live in a broken world with all its pain and suffering. To help get a grasp on the whole passage, I offer this outline.

I.   The Pain (v. 18–17)

The idea of suffering throws many into unbelief in the biblical view of an almighty and good God. If God is almighty, why cannot He just prevent the pain or at least stop it? And if He is good, why wouldn't He? Many wrestle with this, even in the church. But the Bible has answers to this. Many are given in this passage.

First, the pain will not last. It is called "the sufferings of this present time." There will come a time when there will be no more pain for the elect of God. "And God will wipe away every tear from their eyes; there shall be no more death, nor sorrow, nor crying. There shall be no more pain, for the former things have passed away" (Rev. 21:4). The pain now is *not worthy to be compared to the glory which shall be revealed in us*, Paul writes. The pain is not permanent. It will not last. Until then creation suffers under the curse of sin, and as such, we feel the pain of the Creation (Rom. 8:19–22) and the pain because we are Christians (v. 23–27).

When you are in pain it is hard to wait. *Hope* helps us *eagerly wait for it with perseverance*. The *it* there is our salvation, the redemption of our bodies and the end of all pain. God helps us either escape the pain or endure the pain by His Spirit in us and our High Priest interceding for us in the heavens. Christ is in us, and we are in Christ. The Spirit in us helps us pray during this time (v. 26), and the Savior "makes intercession for the saints according to the will of God."

The waiting during the sufferings of this present time is for a good purpose. Why doesn't God just do away with all the pain and suffering for His children in this world? The answer is given in 2 Peter 3:8–9. It has to do with the long-suffering of God. He's waiting, not willing for any of His elect to perish but that all should come to repentance. Jesus will put a stop to all the pain for His own when He comes back, but He won't come back until all the ones He suffered for have repented. If Jesus had come back on June 21, 1969, I would be in hell right now because I was saved on June 22, 1969. So all the Father has given to Jesus have not yet repented, so He waits. This waiting time is the time of our present suffering.

It helps to know that God is not the cause of our pain. He is not the pain giver; He's the Pain Taker. He didn't break your heart by the devastation that came into your life. Jesus said, "I have come to heal the broken hearted" (Luke 4:18). He doesn't break people's hearts; He heals them. Don't blame Him or get mad at Him because you think He has done you wrong or caused you to suffer. Even Job didn't do that (Job 1:22). He is not the cause of suffering; He's the Savior of those who suffer. He doesn't hurt people; He helps and heals people. He is not the god of death; He is the Resurrection and the Life.

II. The Providence (Rom. 8:28–30)

God takes the pain in your life and works it for your good, if you are among those who love God and are fitting into His purpose. That's what God by His providence does in the lives of every believer. What is the good toward which Providence works all things? "He also predestined to be conformed into the image of His Son, that He might be the firstborn among many brethren." He uses everything that happens, the *all things*, to make us like Jesus. His purpose is to fill heaven and earth with people who are like Jesus Christ. Are you fitting into that purpose? Then you can know that the bad things that happen to you will be used for your good.

III. The Proof (v. 31–34)

How do we know God will do all these things? Because He is God and He is for us. How do we know that He is for us? Because of the cross. "He who did not spare His own Son, but delivered Him up for us all, how shall He not with Him also freely give us all things?" This is how we know God loves us and that He is for us. The proof is the cross. If you look anywhere else during the sufferings of this present time, you will be disappointed and confused. Look to Christ *who died, and furthermore is also risen.*

IV. The Peril (v. 35–37)

The *all these things* in which we are more than conquerors are the perils listed in these verses: "tribulation, distress, persecution, famine, nakedness, sword. For Your sake we are killed all day long." While not everybody, thank God, experiences these particular dangers, life is still fraught with perils for everyone. The Bible tells us that the last days will be perilous times, and we are in those.

This is what we must come to grips with—the perils of pain that can cause us to stumble and hinder our living the victorious Christian life that God has for all His children. This chapter is to help us live with the perils and be more than conquerors in those last days.

V.   The Persuasion (Rom. 8:38–39)

What a triumphant way to end this glorious chapter in the Bible! Paul said, "I am persuaded..." Well, if Paul could be persuaded of the things in this chapter, so shall I be. We are safe and secure in the love of Christ. "Nothing can separate us from the love of God which is in Christ Jesus our Lord." We need to know this. Be assured of it. We are secure with God, not matter what. No matter the *sufferings of this present time.*

But we must become persuaded of this. We must become totally convinced of it, no matter what happens to us. This whole passage can be summarized in these few words: *God is for us* (v. 31–34). This is what we must become convinced of. If you are persuaded of this, you will live in victory. You will obey, trust, and enjoy God no matter your adverse circumstances.

Oh yeah! If God is for us, then why is Joseph in this prison in a foreign country? If God is for us, why is Job suffering the loss of his wealth and health and children? If God is for us, then why is Naomi coming back to her hometown of Bethlehem, declaring, "Do not call me Naomi; call me Mara, for the Almighty has dealt very bitterly with me." Doesn't sound like the Lord was for her. But He was. Do you know who that widowed daughter-in-law was who followed her back from the wash pot of Moab? Her name was Ruth. She's the gal who married the richest man in the county. And do you know who their son was? Jesse. And do you know who he fathered? David, Israel's greatest king. Naomi, because of her woes in Moab, was put into the lineage of Jesus Christ. She was blessed, even though she didn't know it at the time.

If God is for us, why is Daniel in the lion's den? Why is Jesus on the cross? Why is Paul in the dungeon? Well, glad you asked. Paul enjoyed God when he was beaten and thrown in prison, because in that dark dangerous dungeon he and Silas sang praises to God (Acts 16). In each of these cases was God for them? Oh yes! Very much so. Don't let your circumstances lie to you about God. He is for you.

1. *You know God is for you because of* the cross, which is God's final answer on that, not your circumstances. "He who did not spare His own Son, but delivered Him up for us all, how shall He not with Him also freely give us all things?" (v. 31–32). Don't let circumstances tell you differently. Faith looks at the cross and not at circumstances. I once ran across a book entitled *If God Loves Me, Why Can't I Get My Locker Open?* It was a book for teens. What a ridiculous idea! Trying to determine if God loves me by whether I can get my locker open or not. Putting that unlocked locker up against the cross! That cross is God's final word about whether God loves me or not. He does. He sent His only begotten Son to die for my sins (John 3:16).

2. *God works everything for your good* (v. 28). This is what it means when it says that God is for me. The sovereign Lord of the universe who controls everything is working all things for my good. It doesn't say all things are good, and it doesn't say all things work to the good of all people. But it does say that all things work together for the good for all those who love Him and are fitting into His purpose. What is the purpose of God, and what is the good toward which all things work? He tells us in the next verses. Ultimately, it is the conforming of all believers into the image and likeness of Christ. God's purpose is to fill the universe with people who think, talk, and act like Him. Nothing can stop the Almighty from pulling that off.

3. *You are foreknown, predestined, called, justified, and as good as glorified* (v. 29–30). It's a done deal, as far as the Lord of the universe is concerned. The language in this text indicates that as many as He foreknew are the same as He glorified. *Foreknew* has nothing to do with God finding out beforehand who would choose Him. The term means to be

intimately acquainted with beforehand. We are considered intimately acquainted with God in eternity past, just as we are now considered glorified in eternity future. From the beginning it has been a done deal. If our salvation from sin is rooted in eternity, then we are secure and we are loved no matter what our circumstances say.

4. *You will never be charged with wrong nor condemned* (v. 33–34). The opening clause in this chapter declares that *there is now no condemnation to those who are in Christ Jesus.* Why? Because Jesus has taken all the condemnation upon Himself. There is no more for you or me. And there never will be.

5. *Nothing can separate you from the love of Christ* (v. 35–39). *Nothing!* Not anything. Nada. I am persuaded of this. "Jesus loves me this I know, for the Bible tells me so." And I am secure in His love. He will never let me go. He loved me while I was still a sinner, and will He love me any less now that I am His child? If I didn't do anything to obtain God's love, it stands to reason that I can't do anything to lose it. Nothing shall separate us from the love of God in Christ Jesus. This is not the generic love of God for all people, people who perish. This is a verse of eternal security. Nothing can separate me from the love of God in Christ Jesus.

To live the Christian life, we need to become persuaded of these things. Life can get you down. These truths can lift you back up and keep you up. Paul was persuaded and so should you be.

This is how you live the Christian life. The *normal Christian life* is a life of conquering all things that come against you. You do that through Him who loved us and gave Himself for us. You do that through becoming persuaded that He is working all things for your good, that God is for you, that He has freely given you all things, that He has elected you and justified you so that He will never charge you with wrong, that He is ever making intercession for you at the right hand of God, and that nothing can ever separate you from the love of

God in Christ Jesus. That is how you live the life of victory! Victory is when you can trust, obey, and enjoy God in all things at all times.

- We will be delivered from all pain (Rm. 8:18–25), and there is help with it even now (v. 26–28).
- We have *hope*, and we have *help*.
- Because of all of this we know that *God is for us*.

HOW TO LIVE THE
CHRISTIAN LIFE

More Than Conquerors

*In all these things we are more than conquerors through
Him who loved us and gave Himself for us.*
—Romans 8:31–39

If we are going to live the Christian life, we must come to terms with
the God who has become our Savior and the suffering in our lives.
We must maintain victory in the mist of afflictions and disappointments with the way things are going at any given time. Romans 8:37
is the greatest verse in the Bible on *victory*. Note the words, "Yet in all
these things we are more than conquerors through Him who loved
us." The all these things of verse 37 are the all things of verse 28, and
they relate directly to the sufferings of this present time of verse 18.
*Victory is trusting, obeying, and enjoying God in all circumstances, even
and especially in bad circumstances.* If you are not doing these three
things, you do not have the victory. If you have sin in your life, you
do not have the victory. Victory can be had in all circumstances at all
times with all believers. It is ours because we have it in Christ.

I.   Victory is for everyone who is in Christ.

It is not the will of God for any Christian to live in defeat. In
Christ we can have victory in every area of our lives, even in suffer-

ing, which is the context of this great verse. And we can experience victory even if we have been defeated for years. Israel was in Egypt for over four hundred years, but one day they walked out a free nation. They had the victory. We can also have victory over any and every sin; in every and all circumstances; and over every fear and worry, every addiction, disappointment, failure, frustration, doubt, grief, heartache, and devil. In fact, the greater the struggle, the sweeter the victory. If I could whip my four-year-old grandson in a fistfight, that would be one thing. But if I could whip the heavyweight champion of the world? Well, that would be something else. The point is, in Christ I could. I can have the victory. I can be victorious in anything. I can defeat any opponent.

Jesus didn't die for you and rise from the dead in order for you to live in defeat. When He died, He was purchasing your freedom over everything that could keep you from obeying, trusting, and enjoying God. When He rose from the dead, He was obtaining victory over all things. That's what makes you more than a conqueror.

II.   Victory has nothing to do with your circumstances.

Some may think, "Well, I could have the victory if I were not married to him (or her) or if it wasn't for so and so (kids, parents, classmates, neighbors) or for this or that circumstance in my life." Do you see the "all these things" of 8:37? Do you know what they are? People, circumstances, demons, death, and things like that. Verses 35 and 36 say, "Who shall separate us from the love of Christ? Shall tribulation, or distress, or persecution, or famine, or nakedness, or peril, or sword? As it is written, 'For Your sake we are killed all day long; we are accounted as sheep for the slaughter.'" You don't have circumstances as bad as theirs, and I hope you never do; but Paul had them, and yet in all these things, he wrote, "We are more than conquerors."

Take Jesus for example. Was He defeated in dealing with the people and circumstances surrounding His arrest, trial, beatings, and crucifixion? I think not. Listen to His words at His trial: "Henceforth, you shall see the Son of Man descending from heaven..." And to Pilate, He said, "You have no power over me except that which is given you from above." To the mockers on the cross He said, "Father, forgive them." He had the worst possible circumstances and people in His life. And we have the same victory "through Him who loved us."

In my door-to-door witnessing, I ran across a young lady in Clio, Michigan. She answered the door and stood there talking with me with a five-year-old son at her knee. Within the last year her mother had died, she discovered she had terminal cancer and less than one year to live, and her husband left her, saying he couldn't take all this. But she said she was trusting God and had no fear. She was glowing with joy and confidence as she shared with me how she knew that God loved her. Her glory was in the cross and resurrection of Christ. She was more than victorious. This young lady, in the worst circumstances, had the victory. We too can know this kind of victory.

III. On what then does victory depend?

A five-letter word states what victory in our lives depends on— *faith*. "And this is the victory that has overcome the world—our faith" (1 John 5:4). And not just any faith, it's faith in the Savior, the One who loved us and gave His life for us.

The fact is, you must *choose what you believe*. Either you believe that Jesus loved you enough to die for your sins or you don't believe it. God loves you means that God is for you. According to 8:31–32, you either believe that God is for you or God is against you. You have a choice. You either believe the gospel or you do not. If you believe it, believe it all the way. If you don't believe, then say, "I don't believe," and get on with your miserable life. Paul said in 8:38, "*For I am persuaded…*" You need to be persuaded too.

You might be saying, "You don't get it. If you only knew what I am going through." It has nothing to do with what you are going through or what you have gone through. It has nothing to do with what people have done to you, or what has happened to you, or your circumstances. It has to do with the cross.

Say to yourself, "God is for me." How do you know that? Not because of your circumstances. They change. You have suffered and you will suffer again because you are still part of the old creation and because you are part of the new creation still living in the old creation. You know God is for you because of 8:32: *"He who did not spare His own Son, but delivered Him up for us all, how shall He not with Him freely give us all things?"* The cross is God's final word on how He feels about those who are called according to His purpose.

Or you might be saying, "But I'm such a bad person. How could He be for me?" The cross says that God is for the worst of sinners. The person who wrote Romans 8 called himself *the chief of sinners*. And the one who is writing this study is a far greater sinner than you are, and I know that God is for me and is working all things for my good. I'm persuaded of it. And what makes you so special that God would pick you out and say, "I don't love you. I'm not for you. I love all these other sinners and am for them, some worse than you, but I don't love you and I am not for you." Get serious. Get faith. Believe everything it says in Romans 8:28–39. Believe it is true. Believe it is true for you. When you do you will have the victory.

Verse 37 is the key verse in all of this. It declares that *in all these things* (the flesh, sin, the world, sufferings, death, demons, etc.) *we are more than conquerors through Him who loved us.* It is not the will of God that we live in defeat or disobedience, worry, or fear. We can have "victory in Jesus" in every area of our lives, even if we have not had it for years. The greater the struggle, the greater the victory! We can have victory over any sin, every addiction, disappointment, discouragement, failure, frustration, doubt, grief, heartache, devil, and in every circumstance. When Jesus died, He was purchasing our freedom and our victory over everything that would keep us from obeying, trusting, and enjoying God. That's what makes us *more than conquerors*. He won the battle and gives us the victory. In 2 Chronicles 20 God won the battle against the three alien armies. Israel didn't have to fire a shot, but He gave them victory. This is what Jesus did by His gospel. He defeated all our enemies and gave us the victory.

Victory has nothing to do with our circumstances. This is the common error of thinking for those in defeat: "If it weren't for this circumstance or that person, I could have victory and be happy." This way of thinking is a chain on many a defeated soul. The sword of the Lord cuts that chain. See the *all these things* in verse 37. Do you know what they are? People and circumstances. Go back up to verses 35–36 and read the listing of *all these things*. Through Christ we are *more than conquerors* in the worst of circumstances, even death.

Note the phrase in 8:31 that says, *"If God is for us."* God is *for us!* There's only one thing that will make you think otherwise—adverse circumstances. But look at the adverse circumstances of the early church and remember that *they* were more than conquerors. Was Christ defeated as His enemies had their way with Him? No! He had the worst possible circumstances, and He was more than a conqueror in them. Behold His behavior from the time the troops came for Him in the garden to His last breath on the cross. What a conqueror! And He is in the business of making us to be like Him.

"Okay, if victory doesn't depend on our circumstances, then upon what does it depend?" As I said, *faith.* I'm not making this up. *Faith is the victory that overcomes the world* (1 John 5:4). Modern man is finding out that faith in and of itself is a powerful thing. But when faith is in something powerful, it is that much stronger. Notice the strong thing that our faith is in—*Him who loved us.* We have a choice in what we believe. Either we will believe that Jesus loves us or that He does not. What does it mean that Jesus loves us? It means what it says in verses 31–32. He did not spare His own Son from suffering for us that He might give us all things.

You will either believe that God is for you or that His is not for you. That is a choice. You must choose one or the other to believe, but by all means *get it settled!* Either believe the gospel and have victory or say, "I don't believe it." According to your faith, so will it be unto you. *Be persuaded.* This Scripture will help persuade you.

HOW TO LIVE THE CHRISTIAN LIFE

Triumph in Suffering

*Yet in all these things we are more than
conquerors through Him who loved us.*

—Romans 8:37

Everybody suffers, but not everyone triumphs over them. The "*all these things*" Paul mentions in our text are *the sufferings of this present time* he mentions in verse 18, which includes two kinds: the sufferings of creation and the sufferings of the Christian.

The *sufferings of the creation (8:19–27)* are universal because we are part of the old creation that was cursed because of Adam's sin. All suffering is because of sin: Adam's sin, someone who has sinned against you, or your own sin. Suffering entered when sin entered. There was no suffering in Eden until there was sin. Neither sin nor suffering is the perfect will of God.

This is paramount for so many because they cannot believe in God because "if God is good and God is almighty then why is there so much suffering in this world?" This is a major hurdle to faith for most unbelievers. The Bible right here (and in Romans chapter one) deals with this very thing. The Holy Spirit gives answers to this dilemma. God is not the author of suffering any more than He is the author of sin. The sin of man has caused all this suffering. Romans 1 and 2 calls it "the wrath of God," which is the righteous judgment of God against a rebellious planet.

Besides the sin of Adam and the sins of others against us, we all pretty much pack our own lunch. This new construction worker was eating lunch with his coworkers the first day and said, "I have a bologna sandwich, and I hate bologna. Can anybody trade with me?" Someone traded his roast beef sandwich for his bologna. The second day, same thing. "I hate bologna!" Someone else traded him for a peanut butter and jelly sandwich. The third day, same song, same verse. One fella said, "Hey, man, why don't you ask your wife to pack you a different kind of sandwich for lunch?" He replied, "What wife? I pack my own lunch!" We all pack our own lunch, and much of our suffering we bring on ourselves by our bad behavior and choices. We value healing over health, and when we don't live healthy lives, suffering occurs.

"Your will be done on earth as it is in heaven." There is no suffering in heaven. These are the pains of the Fall and include sickness, accidents, hurricanes, terrorism, death, infirmities. Christians suffer in this because they still live in this old world and in unredeemed bodies. In 8:22 he writes, "The whole creation groans and labors with birth pangs until now." Just to make sure we know that Christians are included in this type of suffering, in the next verse he writes, "Not only that, but we also who have the first fruits of the Spirit, even we ourselves groan..." But Christians do not have to put up with the sufferings of the creation, because Christ has redeemed us from the curse and consequences of sin, having been made a curse for us on the cross. We still experience the sufferings of creation because nobody has it down perfectly. Nobody believes perfectly. We all still fall short of the glory of God. We all need our faith increased.

The *sufferings of the Christian* (8:28–39) is different from the previous kind. They are unique to the Christian. It is suffering because you are a Christian. After verse 30 he is no longer dealing with just suffering because we are part of this old corrupt creation. It is suffering because of persecution. "*We are killed all day long,*" Paul writes. The Christian has enemies during these present-day sufferings. Satan paints a bulls-eye on the backs of Christians, plus there are unbelievers who have not seen the kingdom of God and thus oppose us. Second Timothy 3:12 says, "*If anyone desires to live godly in Christ Jesus, he will suffer persecution.*"

I.   How we respond to suffering will prove whether our faith is genuine or not.

Many converts have a spurious faith that will not save them. They believe for a while but fall away. They become believers considering *the goodness of God* but become unbelievers when they experience *the severity of God* (Rom. 11:22). They believe, but they believe in vain because in a time of suffering, they do not hold fast the word that was preached to them (1 Cor. 15:1–2). These are the ones whom Jesus said, "Hear the word and immediately receives it with joy; yet he has no root in himself but endures only for a while. For when tribulation or persecution arises because of the word, immediately he stumbles" (Matt. 13:20–21). Instead of making them *better*, their misunderstanding of suffering makes them *bitter* against God. We need not live the Christian life stumbling. That's why the Bible encourages us to "not despise the chastening of the Lord, nor be discouraged when you are rebuked by Him; for whom the Lord loves He chastens and scourges every son whom He receives" (Heb. 12:5–6).

II.   Three things we need to know about suffering.

A.   *Saints do suffer.* This needs to be said. It needs to be received as revelation. Which Bible character did not suffer? (Acts 7:52). The best man who ever live suffered like no other, the holy One of God (Ps. 34:19, Rom. 8:17, 1 Pet. 1:11). Second Peter 2:19–21 says that we were called to *suffer wrongfully*, to *do good and suffer*, if we take it patiently because that is the example set for us by Jesus! "For to this you were called, because Christ also suffered for us, leaving us an example, that we should follow His steps." This is where WWJD came from. What Would Jesus Do? He would take the suffering patiently and forgive those who caused His suffering. That's exactly what He did.

It is the will of God that Christians suffer. Temporarily for sure, but for their own good and God's glory, it is ordained. No pain, no gain. No cross, no crown. We must endure hardship as good soldiers of Jesus Christ. Do not think it strange therefore when you go through periods of suffering. Every human relationship will end in pain. But that's the point: to love someone so much that it hurts when you lose them. Better to have loved and lost than to never have loved at all. Love hurts, just ask Jesus. But there is a resurrection on the other side of your suffering. The glory follows the sufferings of this present time. How helpful it would be if you would just realize that Christians do suffer. It's a fact of life. Settle it in your mind.

B. *God uses suffering* to sanctify His people and make us useful in His service. That's what Hebrews 12:5–11 teaches. Sanctify means to be made like Jesus. When suffering has served this purpose, it will be done away with. In the Bible suffering seems to be synonymous with sanctification. Even Jesus was "made perfect" through the things He suffered, made a perfect Savior (Heb. 2:10, 18).

We are perfected as saints through things we suffer, if we suffer in faith. It is doubtful that God has ever used anyone who has not experienced periods of pain. And it seems the more we suffer, the more useful we are to God. "For the sufferings of Christ abound in us, so our consolation also abounds through Christ. If we are afflicted, it is for your consolation and salvation" (2 Cor. 1:4–7).

I know the victorious handling of my own sufferings have preached better sermons for people than my mouth ever has. God uses adversity, problems, pain, heartaches, and sufferings to grow and mature us into the likeness of Christ; and so we can minister encouragement and comfort to others who are experiencing their own afflictions.

C. *God will ultimately deliver us from all suffering.* The Christian suffers in hope. If we suffer with Him, we will also be glorified together with Him (v. 17). God does now (temporarily) and will ultimately deliver His people from all suffering. People often ask me, "If God is good and almighty, why doesn't He remove Satan and suffering from the earth?" He fully intends to, one day. But until then He uses it to judge the wicked and discipline His people. God removes it automatically for all His people at their death and by the prayer of faith until then. "Is any suffering? Let him pray. And the prayer of faith shall raise him up" (James 5:13–15).

Paul says in the passage, "We are children of God, and if children, then heirs—heirs of God and joint heirs with Christ, if indeed we suffer with Him, that we may also be glorified together" (8:17). Note the "*if.*" We are heirs of God—*if we suffer.* We will be glorified together with Him—*if we suffer with Him.* No cross, no crown. No suffering, no glory. Our experience is to match His, as in "the sufferings of Christ and the glories that would follow" (1 Pet. 1:11). Salvation is our becoming like Christ, and that certainly includes suffering.

Read the whole last half of Romans 8 and you will see that the sufferings of this present time are only for a time. There's a reason the inspired writer uses the expression, "the sufferings of this present time." This present time is only for the present. Whatever suffering you are going through as a Christian will not last. We live the Christian life in hope. Our sufferings are only for a time. An eternity of joy and pleasure is coming.

III. The *help* the Christian has in the sufferings of this present time.

A. We have the *knowledge* that we are children of God (8:14–17).
God is really talking about sons of God when He talks about suffering here: "These are the sons of God...

you received the Spirit of adoption...we are the children of God, and if children, then heirs." The Father did this with Jesus just before he sent Him out into the wilderness to suffer the attacks of Satan. Christ is baptized, the Spirit descends upon Him, and the Father speaks from heaven, *"This is My beloved Son"* (Matt. 3:17). **Then** Jesus is led by the Spirit into the wilderness. He evidently needed to be reminded of His sonship before He suffered. So do we. Suffering doesn't mean we are not sons. It could mean we are!

B. We have *hope* (8:17–25).

Romans 8:17 is a transition that introduces the subject of suffering in the life of the believer. It is amazing that sin should be a part of the believer's life (Romans 7), but it is perhaps even more amazing that suffering would be a part of it! Yet it is. But in Christ and by His Spirit we overcome sin and suffering. Those who suffer with (because of) Christ will *also be glorified together* with Him at our resurrection.

If we suffer with Him, we will be glorified with Him. The suffering will be followed by the glory. The suffering won't last. *Glory shall be revealed in us* after the suffering. "God subjected the creation in hope and the creation itself also will be delivered; we ourselves groan within ourselves, eagerly waiting for the adoption, the redemption of our body, for we were saved in this hope." We have hope. The suffering won't last.

Don't you feel that you could endure almost anything if you knew it wouldn't last? You can endure the night of suffering because you know the morning of joy is coming. The sun will shine again. The day is coming when all suffering will cease; all pain will be in the past; and there will be no more tears or disappointment, sorrow, or night. The pearly gates of God will close on the age of suffering. Good riddance.

The term *adoption* in verse 23 is a reference to the redemption and resurrection of our bodies. When that happens, Christ's millennial kingdom will be instituted on the earth. This is our hope and the hope of the world. Meanwhile, both we and the rest of creation groan under the sufferings of this present time. And we pray. Our groanings are produced by our sufferings and by the Spirit who intercedes for us according to God's will.

C. We have two *intercessors* to sustain us in our suffering (8:23–270).

Intercessors are advocates, lawyers, mediators, helpers. They represent us before a judge, like in a court of law. The Christian has two, two members of the Trinity no less. The Holy Spirit intercedes within us, helping us to pray the will of God, and Christ intercedes for us in heaven because He knows what the mind of the Spirit within us is. *The Spirit intercedes in us, and Christ intercedes for us.* These are powerful intercessors. Our prayers in themselves are powerful weapons during our sufferings. Jesus needed to pray for three hours before suffering on the cross. Prayer helps.

Besides our own prayers, we have two powerful Persons praying for us, and the Father always hears Their prayers and agrees with Them. Hallelujah! The *Spirit* helps our weaknesses by knowing how to pray for us. He makes intercession for us with groaning, which cannot be uttered (v. 26). This can be praying in tongues, but not necessarily. It says, "That cannot be uttered." Tongues are uttered. These prayers are groanings too deep and painful for words. God hears these prayers. And *Christ* **makes intercession for the saints according to the will of God.** We have the two most powerful, compassionate people in the universe in our corner. This is our help in time of suffering. We have the Holy Spirit and Christ Jesus to sustain us. We have hope and we have help.

D. We have the *providence* of God making all things work for our good.

"And we know that all things work together for good to those who love God and who are the called according to His purpose" (Rom. 8:28). This is one of the helps that are given to us in light of "the sufferings of this present time." We have the witness of the Spirit that we are children of God and heirs of God. This helps when we are under the gun of trying times.

Suffering doesn't mean that God has turned against us; it is a good sign that we are indeed His children headed for an inheritance that cannot be compared to our present sufferings. And we have hope—that is, the sufferings won't last. We will not always live in unredeemed bodies and a sin-cursed world. One day the pearly gates will close behind us as we enter the land of "no more." There'll be no more sorrow, pain, death, or suffering. We can endure almost anything if we know it won't last. Thirdly, we have the ever-present help of prayer and the fact that Christ is our Intercessor before the very throne of God in heaven's Holy of Holies. Now we come to *the providence of God that gives us the knowledge that God makes all things that happen to us work out for our good.* What solid bedrock of truth upon which to build the house of our lives. No matter what happens to you, God will use it for your good.

HOW TO LIVE THE CHRISTIAN LIFE

Present Your Body to Christ and the Church

*I beseech you therefore brethren, by the mercies of God,
that you present your bodies a living sacrifice, holy,
acceptable to God, which is your reasonable service.*
—Romans 12:1–21

What's next? Now that God has showered His mercies upon you, what do you do now? Now that God has forgiven you and made you His forever child, what's next on the agenda? How should you respond?

Don't determine that by what others do, because most people have their own ideas about what you do next. And their ideas are mostly wrong! If you get or have an idea that didn't come from God it will be wrong, you can count on it. Isaiah 55 says, "My thoughts are not your thoughts and My ways are not your ways." We need to find out what's next—from God! What does He say we should do next? Live the Christian life. Right, but how do we do that? That's what this series of lessons is all about. But where do you start that? What is the next thing that God wants you to do after you are saved? What does He want you to do? After such mercies have been shown to you, it's the only reasonable thing to find out what you can do for Him, how He would like for you to respond.

Like the first steps of a baby, the first thing is very important, extremely important. What is that first step? The first thing God

125

wants you to do is something you can't do. Not by yourself. He wants you to be baptized in water. That's a passive verb, which means it's something that is done to you, not something you do. Repent and be baptized. Whoever believes and is baptized. That's the scriptural order. The first thing you are to do after the mercy is to find a body of believers to baptize you. This is crucial. You must put your life into the hands of another person, a fellow believer. You must find a church to baptize you. God wants you joined to a body of believers and to show that by putting your life into their hands.

Some people are afraid to be baptized because it looks dangerous. It's supposed to look dangerous. It pictures a burial. You put your very breath in the hands of others. That's the amazing part of Act 2. The apostles baptized three thousand people who had just crucified Jesus! Now they were being commanded to put their lives into the hands of His followers and be baptized in the name of the Jesus they had just been a part of crucifying.

In a series of lessons on how to live the Christian life, what we learn in Romans 12 is an absolute must. Pay attention to this passage of Scripture like your life depended on it, because it does. You cannot possibly live the Christian life without doing what is taught here. It *is* the Christian life. Anything else is not. It is easy to be deceived about this, and many are. They think they can live for Christ without doing these two things.

The first thing to note is that what we have here are instructions on how to live the Christian life. The word of God gives us the how-to here. These things we must do, or we cannot live the life. This passage is filled with verbs, commands for us to obey. Verses 1–21 are not optional, especially verses 1–13. Present your bodies, think soberly, minister the gifts, love, serve the Lord, rejoice, continue steadfast in prayer, bless, weep, associate with the humble, live peaceably with all men, feed your enemy, overcome evil with good. This is the Christian life. It should be memorized and meditated upon, learned and lived. This is how we live the Christian life.

But before we get to the doing, we are reminded of the doctrine. All these commands are the God-ordained response to the mercies of God. *What do you do after you are saved by mercy? You serve.* You serve God and the church. Many never serve in the church. It may be because they have never known the mercies of God. *The only proper response to the mercies of God is to present your body to God and the church.*

First, the word, then the work. First the belief, then the behavior. Don't try to do without first remembering the mercies. "I beseech you by the mercies of God." Imagine God beseeching people. Beseech means to beg. "I beg you by My mercies…" "I plead with you…" What humility from God. Picture the father in the story of the prodigal son going outside and pleading with his elder son to come into the house and join the family in celebrating the return of his brother. Picture God begging us to do something. That's what is going on here. We called upon God for mercy, and He gave us everything we don't deserve. "God, have mercy on me, a sinner," the publican said. And God had mercy on him, and he left church that day justified in the eyes of God.

Those many mercies have been expounded for us in the first eleven chapters of Romans. We were depraved dead sinners (3:10–12), but God had mercy on us (3:21–26). He justified us through faith and forgave us all our sins (4:5). He sanctified us by the death and resurrection of His Son. He delivered us from our sins (Rom. 6), and He delivered us from the law (Rom.7). I tell people, first Jesus saved me from sin and then he saved me from religion. He put us into Christ and the Spirit of Christ into us (Rom. 8). He has worked everything in our lives to make us like Jesus, the very purpose of salvation. He has foreknown, predestined, called, justified, and glorified all those in Christ (8:29–30). He has declared Himself for us by delivering up His Son to save us (8:31–32). He has kept us by His power so that nothing can separate us from the love of God in Christ (8:35–39). And finally, He has given us the perfect illustration of all this in His dealings with Israel (Rom. 9–11). Those are the mercies of God 12:1 is talking about which we are to always remember and never lose sight of. These are the mercies that have made it possible for us to life the Christian life.

What are we to do now that God has poured out His mercies abundantly on us? We are to present our bodies to God and the church for service. That's what Romans 12 is all about. We are to live the life He has purchased and has given to us, and we cannot do that without serving God and the body of Christ.

I.   Present Your Body to God (12:1–2)

Casting Crowns has a song entitled "All He Ever Wanted Was My Heart." Well, that's just not correct. He wants our bodies too, this passage declares that. We cannot serve God and the church without our body. Therefore, we are to present our bodies to them. You cannot serve God without your body. You can't sing, you can't give, you can't teach or anything without your body. We are the body of Christ, bone of His bone and flesh of His flesh. We are the body of Christ. We serve God with our body.

We will not do this if we follow the world. Therefore, we are told not to be conformed to the world. Don't let the world fit you into its mold. Instead, be renewed in the spirit of your mind. Only by doing this will you be living the Christian life. The world thinks little of the church, and sadly, the professing church thinks little of it too. Break the mold. Present your body to God for service. After all the mercies, it's the only reasonable thing to do. What could be more reasonable than that, after all the mercies God has shown to us?

The number one thing Christians want to know and are curious about is the will of God. We ought to want to know and do the will of God. This passage tells you what the will of God is. It is to *present your body to God for service.* You can't get any clearer than that. Present your body for service and our mind for renewing to God. Your mind needs to be renewed by the word of God because you will never think correctly on your own. Your mind must be renewed. You must listen to God and not the world. You must be saved from the world, not have it put you into its mold. The world will never think highly of the church, but Christ died for the church and the church is the body of Christ. This is the will of God for your life. Does that sound reasonable? Yes, it does!

II.   Present Your Body to the Church (12:3–13)

The same epistle that expounds *the mercies of God* in Christ to us follows that up immediately with a command to present your body to God and then a lengthy passage about the church. We are to present our bodies to the church.

Most people miss this. Don't you be one of them. Break the mold. After God has mercy on us, we are to serve Him in the church. Just before I taught this lesson to the church, a man called me and as we were talking he asked me what I was going to teach on. I told him, "How to Live the Christian Life: Present Your Body to God and the Church." He immediately said, "Well, I can see how to live the Christian life, you must present your body to God but what does presenting your body to the church have to do with living the Christian life?" I told him what he said represents most of the church world. They are ignorant of the Bible doctrine of the church. And I told him he needs to read the *Bible*, and he should start with Romans 12, which is one of the many places the importance of the church is stressed.

You can't live the Christian life without the church. I know people say they can, but they are wrong. There are thirty-one "one anothers" in the New Testament and all of them can only be done in the church. We have several of them in the very passage we are covering in this lesson. That's thirty-one commands from God that you cannot possibly obey unless you are involved in the church! So how could you live the Christian life if you do not obey these commands?

We will not do this if we think too highly of ourselves: "I am too important to serve others. God, yes, but not the church." But the mercy of God has placed us in the church: "So we, being many, are one body in Christ." If you are not connected to the body of Christ, how can you possibly do what it says in Romans 12:4–18? You can't.

Our service in the church is not laborious. We serve with the *gifts* of the Spirit, those supernatural enablings. And we do it in *love*. How can we say we love God when we don't love others He has had mercy on? *We can't serve God without serving His church.* So go to the employment office and present your body. You can be without a job, but you need never be without work. Find a place to serve. *That is the will of God.* The Christian life is living the will of God

HOW TO LIVE THE
CHRISTIAN LIFE

Faith and Believing:
Isaac and Jacob

The new pastor preached his first sermon on "Making Disciples." He preached it six times! The elders came to him and asked if he had another sermon and the young pastor replied, "Yes I do, and I will preach it as soon as the church members begin making disciples!" You might want to read this chapter six times, as many as it takes to learn it and live it. It's that important. Do not leave this book until you have faith and are believing, until you have what you have already acquired from the Lord. Only when it is practiced is it practical; only when you access and live off your riches will they do you any good. Isaac lived off the wealth of his father Abraham, and we must live off the wealth of our Father in heaven.

I have saved the best for last. This remainder of this book can change your life for the good forever. You can go to heaven traveling coach or first class. If you've ever done much long-distance flying, you know the huge difference between the two. If you get this down, you will move into first-class flying. Enjoy your flight.

Nothing is more important than faith and believing. Love is greater but not more important. We know the love of God by having faith and believing in God. Without faith it is impossible to please God. We are saved by faith. Never does the Bible say that we are saved by loving. But it does say, "Believe on the Lord Jesus Christ and you will be saved." And "By grace you have been saved through faith." And "The just shall live by faith." We get nowhere with God without faith and believing. John 3:16 is important: "For God so loved the world that He gave His only begotten Son, that whoever believes in Him should not perish but have everlasting life." The importance of faith and believing can be seen throughout the Bible, even from the first pages of Genesis. Nothing illustrates both of these quite like the lives of Isaac and Jacob.

Some things are more important than others. Carrots are more important than candy. Candy is important, but other things are more necessary to life. Coffee is more important than candy. Werewolves would disagree, but the sun is more important than the moon. Some things in the Christian life are like that. Knowledge of Christ is more valuable than knowledge of Queen Esther. She is huge, but Christ is bigger. You can be saved without even knowing there was such a person as Esther but not so with Christ. "God our Savior desires all men to be saved and to the knowledge of the truth." What truth? The next two verses tell us: "For there is one God and one Mediator between God and men, the Man Christ Jesus, who gave Himself a ransom for all..." (1 Tim. 2:3–6).

What I am going to cover in the last part of this book taken from Genesis are two of the most important, if not the most important, things you could ever learn. Don't read this lightly. Your life depends on the truths you are about to read. Reread them. Study them. Learn them. They will make a difference in your life, like the difference between poverty and wealth, sickness and health, love and loneliness.

HOW TO LIVE THE CHRISTIAN LIFE

What We Have Already Acquired from the Lord

And Abraham gave all that he had to Isaac.
—Genesis 25:5

Abraham was rich. "The Lord has blessed my master greatly, and he has become great; and He has given him flocks and herds, silver and gold, male and female servants, and camels and donkeys" (Gen. 24:35). And Abraham had many sons. After Sarah died, "Abraham again took a wife..." and she bore him many sons. But to these many other sons of his second wife and other concubines "Abraham gave gifts to the sons of the concubines which Abraham had; and while he was still living, he sent them eastward, away from Isaac his son" (Gen. 25:1–6). But Abraham gave the inheritance and blessing of God's covenant to Isaac. He alone was Abraham's heir.

Isaac is a character in the Bible that didn't *do* much of anything. He didn't earn anything, go anywhere, was never told to leave his home or do any hard thing that would require faith. He didn't even choose his own wife. He did open some wells, which is important in the Middle East, but he only reopened ones that his father had already dug. It's not what he did that's important so much as who he was. Who he was and what he received is the lesson of his life to us. He teaches us what faith is and what faith believes and receives.

Faith is a noun and believe is a verb. These are important distinctions. Faith is not something we do, it is something we receive. It is a revelation from God. It is substance, spiritual substance, according to Hebrews 11:1. In each of the characters in the Hebrew hall of fame, we see that they got a revelation from God. God spoke to them about something. He gave them information and instruction. That was the revelation. "Faith comes by hearing, and hearing comes by the word of God." Faith comes. God makes the revelation come to us. What we do with that revelation is believe it.

Believe is something we do. It is a verb. We believe the revelation. When we believe the revelation, we please God. Everything depends on our believing what God says and shows us. Sometimes the revelation comes through visions and dreams, but mostly by God speaking to our hearts. God can use anything to speak to our hearts, even a donkey or rooster. What we believe makes us believers. We must believe what God says, or we will believe something contrary to that, and that is not good.

"Father Abraham had many sons; many sons had father Abraham." We sing that, and it is true. But as far as God is concerned and as far as the promises of God are concerned, Abraham only had one son. His name was Isaac. Abe gave all his sons gifts, but then he sent them away! But his inheritance was given only to Isaac. He was not a son of the flesh; he was the child of promise. Father Abraham gave Isaac everything.

Abraham's Isaac is our Jesus. God only has one "only begotten Son." God the Father has given all He has to Jesus. He is God's heir. But here's the thing: we are joint heirs with Christ. "The Spirit Himself bears witness with our spirit that we are children of God, and if children, then heirs—heirs of God and joint heirs with Christ…" (Rom. 8:17). We, being in Christ, get all He has.

All those in Christ have acquired everything. All things are yours. "For all things are yours: whether the world or life or death, or things present or things to come—all are yours" (1 Cor. 3:21–22). This would include the church with all its help: government (Heb. 13:7, 17) and gifts (1 Cor. 12–14). We have been granted all things that pertain to life and godliness (2 Pet. 1:3). We are blessed with every Spirit blessing in the heavenly places in Christ (Eph. 1:3). This includes sonship (God is our Father and we are His children), the Holy Spirit's presence and power in our lives, the forgiveness of all our sins, eternal life, purpose that includes power to have dominion in the earth and bring the kingdom to other people's lives, healing of our mind and body, and deliverance from all spiritual forces of wickedness that bring us into bondage to destructive addictions.

We are righteous, rich and free, joint heirs with Christ so that everything God has we have. I'm talking right now! Right where you sit. We already have these things. The only thing we must wait for is a glorified resurrected body. There is nothing else God has that we don't now have as a present possession.

But you can be filthy rich and live in poverty. Many have done this. I read about an old Native American man who died of starvation on his little Oklahoma farm, when years before he had received a certified letter telling him there was oil beneath his property. He couldn't read. He tossed the letter. After he died, the grandkids let them drill and lived in absolute wealth after that.

You can be a prince and live as a pauper. Two ways you can do this. One, you are ignorant of the last will and testament that God put you into (Heb. 9:16–22). Christ died and left you in His will. Then He rose again to let you know you have everything He has. You just have not known it. Well, now you know. You are as rich as God. He left you in His will. He has given you everything. We are "heirs of God and joint heirs with Christ" (Rom. 8:17). You have everything the wealthiest person in the universe has. You are a joint heir with Christ. Don't you think it's about time you started living like it? The second way you could be rich and not live like it is, you don't know how to access what you have acquired.

You don't know how to get to it or get it into your hands. In that case, simple instructions should suffice. But these simple instructions require the grace of God to follow. They are not easy. Not because God is making it difficult. He wouldn't do that. He wants you to have what He paid for by the shedding of His blood. The difficulty is ours. Because of our unredeemed body that loves carnal worldly things and doesn't want to believe God, we find it hard to live the

Christian life, even though it is so rich. That's why Jesus said the first two things we must do to follow Him is to *deny ourselves and take up our cross daily* (Luke 9:23).

This is what separates the men from the boys, the weak from the strong, the poor from the rich. Millions may know what they have in Christ, but only dozens live like it. The main reason for this is, they don't know what it takes on their part to acquire what they already have. The water is in the well; they just don't know how to get it out. They remain thirsty because they don't know about the bucket and the dipper. The money is in the bank; they just don't know how to draw it out. The information is in the computer; they just don't know the password. They have the car; they can go anywhere they want; they just don't know how to drive it. Do you want to learn what it takes to live like a king's kid, to come out of the slums and live the palace?

HOW TO LIVE THE CHRISTIAN LIFE

How We Possess What We Have Acquired

Jacob said, "I will not let You go unless You bless me."
—Genesis 32:26

The simple answer is, we inherit everything when we are born into the family of God. We earn nothing. Everything is a gift from God. We are born rich toward God, with every spiritual blessing. "Blessed be the God and Father of our Lord Jesus Christ, who has (already) blessed us with every spiritual blessing in heavenly places in Christ" (Eph. 1:3). "His divine power has (already) given us all things that pertain to life and godliness" (2 Pet. 1:3). We have all things. We have everything that Jesus has. We were born rich. We get everything because we were born again in Christ.

Jacob was born heir to everything Isaac had. He was not the firstborn, but the prophecy came: "The elder shall serve the younger." But Jacob didn't believe that promise, so he proceeded to connive and finagle his way to obtain what God had already given him. Consequently, because he didn't believe God, he lost it all and found himself in a foreign land away from the land of promise and his father's house and inheritance. Then he returned home, only to receive word by his scouts that his offended brother Esau, who was last seen trying to kill Jacob, was coming to meet him with an army. Jacob could always run, and so he sent everything to Esau and took off running. But God arrested him, put his hip joint out of socket, and then said, "Good-bye!" Jacob was at the end of himself. He could not run from his brother, and God was leaving him. That's when he believed. That's when his believing kicked in. He grabbed hold of God and wouldn't let him go. He said, "I will not let you go until you bless me." And God did bless him. Changed his name to fit into his inheritance and changed Esau's heart toward him. Jacob believed. *This is what believing looks like. It says, "I will not let God go until he blesses me, until I get what He promised."*

We are born again by the sovereign Spirit ministering the word of truth to our hearts. We come alive to God by the quickening power of the Holy Spirit. He who has the Son has life. Once we are saved, the one word that sums up our responsibility in acquiring what we have is the word *believe*. But that word is easily misunderstood, and I fear is by most. That misunderstanding makes us live in poverty, even though we are heirs of God. Biblical believing is not a thing that merely happens in our heads. We don't just believe the facts stated in the Bible. The demons believe all that, and they are not heirs of God. We can believe in vain, and through that believing get nothing.

My aim in this lesson is to tell you from the Bible what the word *believe* means. It is a multifunctional term that carries many meanings. We get everything God has by believing, so we need to know what believing means. We are saved by believing, healed by believing, set free from addictions by believing, provided for by believing. We get everything we get from God by believing. All things are possible for those who believe. If we are to get any benefit from the word of God, it will only be through believing it.

So what is believing? This is a most understood thing. What if your prayers have not been answered because you are not believing the way the Bible teaches you are to believe? What if the defeat in your Christian life is because you don't know how to believe? This is important.

Faith is the key to life. It's up to each one of us to learn how to use this amazing key to everything. We are told by Jesus to "Have faith in God" (Mark 11:22). We are told that the prayer of faith will save the sick (James 5:15). *The coin of the realm has faith on one side and believing on the other. Faith is the revelation God makes to your heart while believing is what we do with that revelation.*

All the commands God tells us to do, such as praying and fasting and calling for the elders of the church to lay hands on us and anoint us with oil, are merely aids to get us to the point of faith. If we could just believe, we wouldn't need all the other things. We wouldn't need to pray or fast or even have others pray for us. But alas, we find it hard to believe, so we are given things to do that help us get to where we can. But make no mistake about it, we can go directly to "Go" on the Monopoly board without going to jail or taking any detour at all. These aids are precious and powerful, but all they do is get us to the point of faith and believing.

Faith is what the first half of this lesson is about. It's the first thing I covered. We know by faith. It's not enough to simply read, "What We Have Acquired from the Lord," we must have it in our spirit. It must be revealed to our spirit by the Holy Spirit. We must know it by revelation. That is faith. You may need to pray over that truth (as well as any other truth in the Bible), or fast and pray over it, or read and reread the scriptural texts referenced in it; but by all means get it in your heart. It is only then that you can believe. With the things of God, you can only believe what is revealed to your spirit. Ask the Holy Spirit to make this real to you.

So we come to believing. What does it mean to believe something God has told us? *What is involved in believing? Believing is only possible when we hear the voice of God and act on it.* Read the great chapter on faith (Hebrews 11) and see that this is true. By faith Abel offered to God a more excellent sacrifice. By faith Enoch was taken up. By faith Noah, being divinely warned of things not seen, prepared an ark. By faith Abraham obeyed. By faith Isaac blessed Jacob. By faith Moses forsook Egypt. By faith the harlot Rahab received the spies. Faith always produces action. You can't believe something without acting on it.

Jesus showed us what faith is in Matthew15:21–28. A woman went to Jesus for deliverance for her daughter. Jesus ignores her plea, but she pursues Him relentlessly. I do not think He is refusing her. Everything for Him was a teaching opportunity. He's wanting to show the disciples and us something very important here. What would that be? What faith is. He wants us to see what faith does, because He knows how important faith and believing is. We get nothing from God apart from faith. Jesus refused to give her what she wanted. He first ignores her and then seems to insult her: to Him she's like a scavenger dog scouring the neighborhood for scraps. But she never gives up. She argues with Him, answers all His objections until He marvels, gives her what she came for, and declares, "O woman, great is your faith!" *That* is faith. And that's what we don't see in these days of the quick fix. Most people would quickly say, "Well, that didn't work," and walk away with their prayer unanswered. To believe means to not stop till you get what God has given you.

Time and time again Jesus would say, "According to your faith let it be unto you." In one place He even said, "All things are possible to him who believes" (Mark 9:23) So what are you believing God for? Maybe the better question is, "What are you wanting to believe God for?" Healing for your body? Healing for a loved one's body? Salvation for yourself or for someone else? Whatever it is, get ahold of God and say what Jacob said, "I will not let you go until you bless me." Do what the widow did with the judge: "And shall God not avenge His own elect who cry out day and night to Him." Jesus closed that story about "men always ought to pray and not lose heart" with these words, "When the Son of Man comes, will He really find faith on the earth?" (Luke 18:1–8). Do what the neighbor did when he needed food and the man wouldn't give him any but finally did "*because of his boldness*" (Luke 11:5–8).

Finally, Jesus is teaching us this very thing in His excellent instructions on prayer in Luke 11:9–13 where He said, "Ask and it will be given to you…" The verb tense here in the Greek language indicates it is a continuous action. Keep on keeping on, which is the very point of the preceding parable. He who keeps on asking will be given. He who keeps on seeking will find. So don't stop. Never give up. What do you have to lose, except your life or your soul?

Believe the revelation that you are a joint heir of God with Christ and that everything He has is yours. And based on that, begin to receive what you know He has given you. And never stop until you have it. Do not let God go until He blesses you.

We live the Christian life by faith. "The just should live by faith." Those who are right with God live by faith in God and His word. We believe, and we continue to believe until we obtain what Christ has purchased for us on the cross.

I want to close this study on How to Live the Christian Life with the most important lesson of all. To do that I will answer this vital question: "Does God ever say no to us?" Does He ever not answer our prayer? Yes! There are times when His answer is no. But when He does, it is for a good reason. He has a greater purpose. An example from each of the testaments will help. David's son was sick, very sick. David cried to God day and night. He refused to eat or clean up. All he did was pray. Finally, the baby died. God had said no to this godly man's persistent prayers. David never felt guilty about any lack of faith. He never condemned himself saying, "I should have done better at this faith and believing thing." Don't ever feel condemned because someone is sick and your prayers are not helping, or because someone dies even though you are trying to have faith and believe God for their healing. David didn't, and neither should you. When David heard that his baby had died, he got up off the floor, ordered something to eat, cleaned himself up, went to church and worshiped God (2 Samuel 12:15–23).

Paul suffered from a thorn in the flesh (2 Corinthians 12:7–10). He prayed and prayed that it might be removed and God said no. Don't stop praying and believing until God says no and you know it, and you know why He said no. The Lord told Paul that His grace was sufficient for him to endure this for the greater good. *"My grace is sufficient for you, for My strength is made perfect in weakness."* What was the greater good? That the power of Christ might be upon this man of God. Paul concluded, *"Therefore most gladly I will rather boast in my infirmities, that the power of Christ may rest upon me. Therefore I take pleasure in infirmities, in reproaches, in needs, in persecutions, in distresses, for Christ's sake. For when I am weak, then am I strong."* If you can live with peace and power in your adversity and give God the glory, then rest with Jesus when He prayed, *"Not my will be done, but Yours be done."*

God was healing lot of people in the church I pastored, but then one of our elders died of cancer. At the funeral I addressed what was on many people's mind. They wanted to know if we were going to continue to believe and preach healing. I declared at that funeral that we were going to believe and practice what the Bible says in spite of what had happened to Tony. His death had changed nothing that was in the Bible. God heals. Period. And He continued to heal people in our church after Tony passed away.

The bottom line in living the Christian life is what Job said, *"Though He slay me, yet will I trust in Him."* (13:15) The words of an old hymn will close our thoughts on this: **"Trust and Obey, for there's no other way, to be happy in Jesus, but to Trust and Obey."**

ABOUT THE AUTHOR

Terry is married to Holli, has four daughters, eleven grandkids, and one great-grandson. He has pastored for forty-nine years, preaching through books of the Bible, chapter by chapter and verse by verse. He has studied Greek and Hebrew in college and seminary. He has always enjoyed working with youth. His specialty is discipling and teaching. Terry has been a missionary for years in Nepal, Kenya, and Honduras. He is a people person and a man of the Bible. Saved in 1969, he immediately began studying and sharing the word. He has been doing so ever since. He is a lifelong student of history and has a bachelor's degree from Grand Canyon University in it. Terry has a love for life, people, and Jesus Christ. He has worked with people and studied the Bible all his adult life.

CPSIA information can be obtained
at www.ICGtesting.com
Printed in the USA
LVHW020740101120
671146LV00007B/406